The Things I Used To Do To Sneeze!

How to Live an Authentic Life

Third Edition

Monica Cost

ISBN: 0984048847
ISBN 13: 9780984048847

ACKNOWLEDGMENTS

To God who kept me alive when I jumped off a moving school bus in the eighth grade, hitchhiked in the ninth grade, was robbed at gunpoint and drank too much in my early twenties, and nearly choked on saltwater taffy in my mid-twenties. For all that you've spared me from, I am grateful.

To my earthly family, I say thank you to my wonderfully strong, courageous, and determined mother for giving me emotional and spiritual support, even when you didn't have anything left to give and for instilling an incredible amount of confidence in me that allowed me to find my voice. **Thank you, Mommy**, for continually supporting this truth journey despite your own wants for me. I love you. Thank you to my eldest son, **Christopher**, for loving me as I learn through my mistakes, for showing me myself, for giving me your compassion, and for inspiring truth every day. Thank you to my youngest son, **Cameron**, for your unwavering congruency, your honesty, your never-ending questions, and your quest for truth at all costs (no pun intended). I love you both immeasurably. Thank you to my sister, **Tiffany**, for sisterhood, for fervent prayers on my behalf, for always seeing the brighter side, and for finding a way out of everything. Thank you for spreading the word about this book like no one else will.

Thank you to my former husband, **Donald Cost**, for being the most amazing father to our sons and for loving them so wonderfully through life's ups and downs. Thank you to all my dear friends who continue to bring amazing balance, support, love, and laughs: **Kevon Edmonds**, for your continued support of the journey. **Tia Ervin**, for listening and offering your guidance during my transition to truth. **Moraima "Mo" Ivory**, for questioning my journey to truth every step of the way, taking me with you, and teaching me how to get the "wristband." **CJ Miller**, for your friendship, exploration of truth, countless brainstorming sessions, and for always inspiring me to write. You are partly responsible for this book being written. **Robyn Muldrow**, for listening and laughing until we cried. **Janay Smith**, for joining me, sometimes unwillingly, on this journey to living truth, for pushing me to try to understand everything on the *table*, and for giving your amazing input to the content in this book; it would not have been the same without you. **Cheryl Spruill**, for your continued support despite your own truth.

Thank you to my angel investor, who believed in me enough to give me wings for the journey out of the "LOMB." To **Bennie Wiley**, for your ongoing inspiration, encouragement, guidance, and support through my many seasons of life. To **Amy Fardella**, for identifying and helping me to understand and utilize "the laser." To **Beverly Edgehill**, my friend and mentor for your unwavering support, honesty, and knowledge. To my phenomenally talented and no-nonsense Line Sisters and Big Sisters of **Delta Sigma Theta Sorority, Inc., Gamma Iota Chapter**, for a life-changing experience and love that will last a lifetime. To my crew of **Milton Academy Moms** (with a special shout-out to **Elaine Blais** for the rescues), who constantly and consistently encourage me in the quest.

Thank you to my Facebook and Twitter family, for listening and sharing your lives with me. To all the seekers, defenders, and maintainers of truth, for not being satisfied with "Living in the LOMB." And finally, to everyone who told me no, thank you for lighting the fire under my behind to write this book.

~ CONTENTS ~

~ CONTENTS ~

The Things I Used To Do To Sneeze

INTRODUCTION

AHHH, AHHHH, ACHOOO! There is nothing like a good hardy sneeze. For as long as I can remember, I have loved the sensation of sneezing. My body shakes, my eyes slam shut, my head jerks forward, and—if I'm standing—one leg pops up in the air. It all ends with a big smile. It is awesome! The physical sensation gives my entire body a treat, and I can't get enough. When I was a girl, I loved sneezing so much that I would sometimes find a way to tickle my nose so I could enjoy this amazing physical sensation.

Speaking of sensations, while pondering how to deliver a message on authentic living, I began thinking about how people long for emotional sensations, much as I did for the physical sensation of sneezing. Similar to the disingenuous process I used to make myself sneeze, sometimes we utilize a disingenuous, or false, process to achieve the emotional sensations we're after. This false process is one that is based on external values, such as those suggested by society, rather than our self-discovered authentic values.

As an example, some of the emotional sensations we chase are the sensations of feeling loved, accepted, acknowledged, considered, and respected. Because of the barrage of external pressures and expectations, the journey we take to achieve these sensations is often inauthentic to who we are at our core. Most of the time, it happens so subtly that we are unaware until the raging sensation of *unfulfillment* creeps in later in life.

Throughout this book, you will see a sensation noted that applies to the circumstance discussed. For instance, the sensation of *having* may have been achieved by foregoing one's authentic value system to have material gain. The sensation of *acceptance* may have been achieved by abandoning one's value system to gain entry into a particular group. Keep in mind that while we often achieve these sensations when we forego our values, the fulfillment we get is temporary. We can still arrive at the same sensations by actually embracing and living out our core values. The point of identifying these emotional sensations is to move us closer to understanding the motivation for our actions.

Instead of obtaining (emotional) sensations authentically, we sometimes tickle our circumstances, much as I tickled my nose, by altering our values; for instance, we change our appearance, claim to agree with circumstances when we actually don't, sacrifice fulfillment for status, gossip, overspend, and more. We spend less time with our families in our quest to gain more material possessions. We push our true friends aside to associate with the "right" network of friends. We ignore the warning signs that tell us our relationship is not working because we are focused on marrying—or staying with—the "right" person. We forego pursuing our passions to follow the expectations put upon us by our parents, teachers, and friends. All of this we do while pretending everything in our life is just as we want it.

When we pursue emotional sensations through processes that are not aligned with our core value systems, feelings of anger, depression, disappointment, guilt, insecurity, jealousy, sadness, and self-loathing often arise. We adopt systems that are buried in what I have named the "LOMB[1]" (Land of Make Believe), a place where truth is based on perceptions and hidden by labels, and most (emotional) sensations are achieved through elements of a false life journey to keep achieving the desired labels.

In the LOMB, it is convenient to apply labels to circumstances based upon what we perceive. For instance, in the LOMB, someone who lives in a particular house, in what may be deemed a coveted neighborhood, may be given the label of *wealthy*. Or a person who has the title of Chief Executive Officer may be given the label of *successful*. In actuality, the labels we apply rarely, if ever, match the person to whom we're affixing them all the time. In addition, the person we're assigning the label to may not define the label

---

1 Pronounced to rhyme with "bomb"

in the same way we do. Oftentimes, the people receiving the labels wouldn't agree with the label given, but at the same time, the pressure to keep those labels becomes overwhelming. At the end of the day, all we really have are the facts or the truth in the moment. CEO is simply a title; we can't assign any labels, like successful, to it after that acknowledgment, unless we know how that particular CEO defines the label we're assigning. We also have to remember that the label we apply does not apply across the board. No one is successful all the time and in every area.

My own label-chasing behavior led me to this place at this time to write this book. After having come face-to-face with the seven truths in my own life, I was ready to share. They are the seven truths that we'll discuss in this book.

I believe it was only after this self-discovery that I could be in a position to spread the L.Y.T.E.[2] (Live Your Truth Experience). The truths came so fast and in so many aspects of my life: aesthetic, relational, spiritual, emotional, financial, professional, and parental. I truly felt as though I were in a crash course on self-discovery. At the end of it, I stood in the pureness of me.

Aesthetic: Despite the positive attention that came from having long, black hair, I aligned with my value of efficiency

---

2 Pronounced as "light"

by cutting my hair and letting the dye go. So I now have short, gray hair; this lets me feel stylish without a lot of bother.

Relational: Despite the "perfect family" label we received, I left a marriage that simply was not working. Now, I am free to love without the external pressures of what it should look like.

Spiritual: Despite the urging from some of my fellow Christians to "leave it alone," I challenged my religious beliefs and came much closer to God. Now I feel more centered in my own spiritual experience.

Emotional: Despite the label of "strong" that I was often given, I addressed my past troubles, learned to accept being vulnerable at times, and gained a greater understanding about my behavior in past relationships. Now I accept my emotional states and am able to work through them in a healthy manner.

Financial: Despite the label of success I often received because of my material possessions and positions, I began to recover from my "shopaholicism" and gained a handle on being financially fiscal. Now, my financial choices stem from my personal goals and not expectations of how I should allocate my resources.

Professional: Despite the positive societal labels and accolades I had received from being the first black woman commercial real estate broker for a major firm in Massachusetts, I quit my corporate job during a recession to run my own business. Now I live my professional truth according to my personal values and mission.

Parental: Despite the social norm of projecting our own thoughts and beliefs upon our children, I embarked on a journey to assist my children in living their most authentic lives. As a result, my children have begun their own personal journey of living according to their values and not the values of others.

* * *

Once I found my way out of the LOMB, I felt a strong desire to share this new knowledge about truly living authentically. As you will learn throughout this book, it is only in the face of self-discovery, understanding, and a commitment to let go of the pursuit of societal labels that you can find your way to you. It is a way of life I can now never cease to live. Once you've gotten a taste of the real you, your appetite for personal truth only grows stronger.

Living your most authentic life requires you to embark upon a "sensation exploration process." This is the process of understanding your emotional desires. Each one of us is chasing a feeling, a *sensation*.

The first step in this exploration process is to identify your core values by asking yourself, *What are my pet peeves?*

This will give you a sense of situations and circumstances that have the potential to derail you emotionally through your response. *What values are important to me?* Understanding your values gives you a sense of how far you are willing to go to achieve your desired sensations. Without them, you can end up very lost. I know from personal experience. *Why are those values important to me? What to those values mean to me?* These last two questions will help you clarify your personal values and to give meaning to them. Not everyone who values connectedness values it in the same way, as an example. The answers to these questions are critical for you to develop your path to achieving the sensations (or emotions) you desire. As a reminder, examples of these are sensations of feeling loved, accepted, acknowledged, considered, and respected. They represent the way you prefer to feel.

The second step is to understand the (emotional) sensations that you want to create in your life. Achieving this step comes by evaluating your answer to the question, *Which feelings bring me the most fulfillment?* For instance, feeling considered is one of my preferred sensations. The answer will give you a clearer understanding of what motivates you. Knowing that one of your top desired sensations is *acceptance* will make it less confusing to your soul when you find yourself experiencing feelings of unfulfillment after making yourself attend a social gathering and still not gaining access to certain connections. The experience of unfulfillment comes when our emotional sensations are not met or when they are achieved by directly challenging our core values.

While it is possible to achieve temporary emotional fulfillment by ignoring your core values, eventually your soul will recognize the disingenuous journey, and it will rebel with feelings of disappointment and more.

The third step is to determine how far you are from living according to your core values by asking, *What do I want out of life, and which values am I currently using to achieve my desired sensations?* I'll go into more detail on sensations and values ahead. Once you determine the answers to these questions, then you are ready to take the final step in the sensation exploration process, which is to put everything into motion and move forward on your path toward an authentic life filled with many awesome sensations.

Throughout the book, you will see callouts that I have named, "Sprinkling Pepper." These are relevant to the chapter and lessons that may be worth referring to later.

Before we begin, let me give you the Reader Beware disclaimer. Reading *The Things I Used to Do to Sneeze: How to live an authentic life* may lead to drastic and life-changing behavior. Some readers have abandoned external expectations and begun to live in their truth. Others have made radical moves that increased their happiness, fulfillment, and confidence, which led them to pursue their true purpose. Read on if you can live with these risks.

It's time to define your truth and live it. Let's go!

~ 1 ~

THE ORIGIN OF
THE MOVEMENT

The Sensation of Transition

I once interviewed the author of a women's empowerment book on the effects of the ever-changing value systems the current generations have experienced—from the baby boomer generation until now. In our conversation, she mentioned that we may have lost something in our value system from generation to generation in our quest to have more, to be better, and to get everything faster.

I believe that what appears to be a loss of values is actually a shift in those general community values to personal core values. One community cannot share an entire set of values and still be true to its individual members. The baby boomers certainly sacrificed more of themselves and their wants for the sake of their families and communities than recent generations. However, I'm not sure that their high levels of personal sacrifice were the best path to a "great" life either. This is a clear example of how the values you're expected to live by according to society are not always in line with who you are.

While I do understand that sacrifice is necessary to achieve harmony at various points in our lives, we must also maintain a balance with our own values. Without this balance, lack of fulfillment is probable, and regret is inevitable. I believe this lack of balance contributes to the high levels of stress many of us are currently experiencing.

The new generation came along after the baby boomers with one goal in mind: to find a new kind of balance. Yes! Generation X (Gen X), also known as the Pepsi Generation, marked a new era in our society. We were the rebels, the original latchkey kids. Our parents gave us room to question the rules, and we changed the game. We decided that loyalty was for those who deserved it, that women should be encouraged and supported if they want or need to work outside of the home, and that families are as individual as we are. If our family needed a non-traditional structure, then we made it happen. We concluded that the status quo was insufficient, and we decided that we simply wouldn't bear the pain that came from doing things "because that's the way they've always been done."

A few corporations saw this trend, and a popular cola company was one such company. The corporate pioneers called it "lifestyle marketing" which was their way of saying, "marketing that appeals to the activities, interests, and opinions of consumers." They created campaigns that included terms like "Feelin' Free," "You've Got a Lot to Live," and others that promoted individuality. Researchers studied the Gen-X children and said, "Something's different about these kids," and they were right! A switch to lifestyle marketing, along with the proliferation of fast food, microwaves, cell phones, and computers, appealed to our budding desire for instant gratification and helped to launch us into a new level of "now." We wanted a better quality of life and faster outcomes, which meant having more time to do the things we wanted to do.

The Origin Of The Movement

Gen Xers began a new movement that has influenced our whole society. Women are more sure and more willing to express themselves. Men are adjusting to a new paradigm, taking ownership over what it means to be active fathers, husbands, and significant others. Girls do not have to keep proving they can achieve because they are displaying their capabilities, and the boys are beginning to recognize it too.

Our feisty generation birthed the quest for a new normal that began with our need to ask why. Why stay at a company where we are not valued? Why must we work long hours without a retirement plan? Why shouldn't women be in the boardroom? Why should we vote for this candidate? Why do we need to marry? Why do we have problems communicating? Why are we together? Why should we go back to the way things were? Why should we follow you? Why?

Generation Xers may experience more reported infidelity, divorce, and job changes than any generation before it, but we've decided that if better is possible, then good is not enough. We ushered in the beginning of a much-needed transition when we forced the world to acknowledge that things did not fit into our new definitions, despite our pretense that they did. We challenged the norms and began to establish new paradigms. We decided to live on our terms, which will one day create a more balanced society. We have made great strides in that direction, but we're not there yet.

We're not there yet, because when people find a new freedom, the freedom and the power that oftentimes comes with it are typically exploited for a period of time. We're finding out what it's like to fly with these new wings of access and what it means to "do me." We've taken full advantage of our options and may have tipped the scale too far in the other direction.

Instead of utilizing our new options and our access to find true balance, we have created new scorecards for success and happiness that now include judging each other by how much and how many. How much "stuff"? How much access? How much influence? How much fame? How many hits? How many friends? How many followers? Unfortunately, the pressure of keeping up hasn't left much time or energy for self-exploration.

So it's difficult to ensure that what we're chasing is really what we want. This dilemma has moved us deeply into the LOMB, a place where the judgment lies in what is seen. Many fall into the trap of believing that if it looks better, it must be better. This level of surface living causes many to continue to chase the labels that come with shallow perceptions. Here we find ourselves going deeper into the rabbit hole of the LOMB.

And where are we now? Well, we want more. More what? More purpose, more understanding, more truth, and more than just what it "looks like" on the surface. We want a higher level of truth in the deep things of life. We want fulfillment.

My hope is that in this new quest for truth, we will stand firmly in our own presence without comparing our lives to others, knowing that on our path we will experience less regret. In this new truth, women and men will find true partnership in marriage and togetherness, and we will all find a deeper purpose. We will look at the content of someone's character to determine that person's place in our lives and not at what he or she has acquired. We will determine our connections based on value alignment and not value perceived. We will buy only what we can actually afford. We will raise our children to focus more on the community and less on the self. And we will emerge as new people, where the truth of who we are is celebrated.

This is what arises when you transition into achieving authentic emotional sensations or feeling the way you prefer to feel the most (for instance, loved, accepted, acknowledged, considered, and respected). You can stand on your own—not anyone else's—values. I liken this process to giving birth, which is analogous with transition. And with birth comes pain. Yes, there will be pain, but don't panic! We are in transition, trying to understand how to live with this new realization, in this new paradigm. You may be searching for a new definition of truth, and once you find and embrace that truth, then you will have opened that door labeled "My Authentic Life."

My primary reason for writing *The Things I Used to Do to Sneeze* is to free you from an unfulfilling life and usher you into a life that is more genuine and purposed. I want to help you live a life true to your values, which will create the most authentic journey to achieve your most desired emotional sensations. In the end, our world will be better because we had the best of you.

* * *

Chapter 1 Reflections

- We're in transition out of the LOMB (Land of Make Believe) and into the LOAT (Land of Authenticity & Truth).

- With transition comes pain, so moving into your authentic life will cause some discomfort.

- A new balance is necessary for us to progress.

- You do not have to live an unfulfilling life.

- Do not worry about labels when you are considering your authentic life.

- Regret is not inevitable.

~ 2 ~

THE BEGINNING OF MY TRUE SENSATIONS

The Sensation of Relief

The Beginning Of My True Sensations

I remember when I made the decision to leave my corporate job at a commercial real estate firm and to take a chance on being a full-time entrepreneur. I desperately wanted to run my pathfinding and strategy firm full-time. After all, I'd spent my whole life up to that point living up to everyone else's expectations. I was polite, a good student, and I chose the major in college that my teachers, parents, and counselors thought was best: finance. I got high grades throughout high school, jobs in finance that paid well above the average, and so on. I was what some would have labeled a "good egg," and I only very rarely stepped out of line or challenged "the system." But now it was time to transition from that safe space to a place that felt more like me, more authentic. Before I could do that, though, I first had to determine who I was and what "authentic" meant to me.

As I expected, when I shared my intentions of leaving my corporate job, many of the people in my circle urged me to reconsider.

"You have a family and a *great* job. Why would you want to risk it when you are doing so well?" they asked.

"I must do it," I responded.

A great job? Sure, if all you count is money and labels. But "great" for whom? My truth for what a great job entailed no longer matched society's understanding of "great." I now know that it never did.

It was at this first big crossroads in my adult life when I realized I had been traveling the wrong path to achieve my desired emotional sensations. And I was unclear about why I was on that path. The journey to the sensations I was craving was not aligned with my true values or my soul.

When I took time to reflect, I realized that the things I was doing, such as working in certain positions, associating with particular people, and attending various "in-the-know" events, were not the way I wanted to achieve the sensations of acceptance, admiration, and recognition. It was also during this time that I began to rediscover facets of myself, and I realized that those facets were related to different values than the ones I was living. They included values that were truer to my core. They were authentic.

I began to try new things and adopted a general openness to a life that had once seemed closed. I became more flexible, more spontaneous, and less conservative. I communicated more openly and stopped feeling obligated to say yes. In addition, I realized that I didn't care as much as I thought I did about perception just for the sake of it, what people thought of my decisions, or whether my life was worthy of the labels others wanted to affix to me. I was beginning to understand what it meant to be truly free. I was coming out of the LOMB.

Unfortunately, the epiphany that I was living in the LOMB—and the changes I would need to make to get out of it—caused quite a stir, not only in my life but also in the lives of the people who were most important to me, like my then husband, my children, my mother, and even some close friends. A few of my religious friends labeled my new-found authentic-living philosophy as selfish, but I called it self-preservation. I later came to recognize it as, "sensation congruency." Being different people in different places was becoming exhausting. I was becoming clearer about why I wanted the sensations I was looking for in life and how far I would go to attain them. I was also beginning to realize the lengths to which I would *not* go, even if it meant never feeling those sensations again. Sensations are tricky and can be addictive. Much like a drug, sensations give you tempo-rary emotional highs until the next situation comes around the corner and doesn't give you the feeling. This is when many of us abandon what we value to chase the high. In true Generation X fashion, I started asking *why*.

I don't remember the moment I began asking that all-too-important question as much as I remember feeling it in my spirit. Initially, I panicked and felt as though I were suf-focating. I was coming to the realization that I no longer fit neatly into the life I was living. From home to work to social situations—the walls were closing in, and I had to figure out how to stop them.

As my awareness of the LOMB grew, I was uncomfortable telling anyone how I felt, especially in the beginning. I'm not even sure I would have known how to describe it, other than to have said, "I feel panicked!" From the outside looking in, I had a great life. In fact, people used to frequently tell me how blessed I was. I knew most of them wouldn't understand why I was looking for something different. By the time I came to realize I was living in the LOMB, I was already eating a nice, big piece of the American pie. While it wasn't a terrible tasting pie, it was missing too many of the ingredients I had discovered I liked.

Now, I don't want you to get the impression that I wasn't experiencing any joy while living in the LOMB. Actually, when you don't know you're there, it's fantastic—for a while. As the saying goes, "ignorance is bliss." I still had lots of good times, laughs, and even personal growth in the midst of the LOMB. But while I felt very fortunate to have my daily comforts, my soul was becoming more and more uncomfortable. When the waters of my life were still, the oil of truth rose to the top, giving me a clear view of the changes I needed to make. My soul cried out for truth and a different path, and this is when I put my real estate in the LOMB up for sale and set out in search of a residence in the LOAT. I was ready to experience a life more in line with my own values, a life where I could "sneeze" authentically and achieve my desired sensations.

* * *

The Truth
My truth begins with me.
When I quiet my soul, my truth I will see.
When I find that truth I've been searching to be,
Will I have the courage to live my truth, or will I flee?

* * *

Chapter 2 Reflections

- Don't ignore your soul's desire for something more.

- If you feel unfulfilled, don't let people convince you everything is OK.

- Living your most authentic life often comes with some discomfort.

- Be respectful of others' opinions, even if you don't agree.

- Remember that most people haven't discovered when or in what ways they are living in the LOMB.

~ 3 ~

EXPECTATIONS AND SENSATIONS

Pressure and Motivation

I began my journey to truth after realizing how far from an authentic life I was living. During this time, I met, spoke with, read about, and watched people living painfully in the LOMB. Some of them were notable personalities who, unfortunately, had their epiphanies about being in the LOMB while in the public spotlight. Some were friends & acquaintances; some were strangers I met along the way who felt compelled to tell me their stories.

We mostly take up residence in the LOMB to appease external expectations. These are expectations to be beautiful, cool, good, wise, lazy (expectations are not always productive), married, straight, successful, thin, and more. Here, truth is an outcast spurned by negative influences. Abuse, childhood experiences, life's circumstances, social pressures, and even the temporary praise we gain from living the lie—all these things and more conspire to relocate truth into the background of our lives. The LOMB does not discriminate. Its residents can be any race, shape, size, gender, or ethnicity. Much as the motto in many churches is "Come as you are," the motto in the LOMB is "Come as you are—we'll do everything we can to keep you here."

Some people choose to live in the LOMB, where they can create their lives with success indicators that are aligned with the mainstream ideals. These indicators tell the outside world in which box to place LOMB residents. Yes, a box. In our society, everyone needs a box, or so we are conditioned to think. It's comfy in there, and it contains all kinds of boundaries to keep us secure enough to be deterred from venturing too far outside of it and possibly wandering into our true purpose.

This is not the way to fulfillment and purpose. People use these false indicators to decide whether they want to label you as poor or wealthy, spiritual or earthly, gay or straight, smart or dumb, successful or unsuccessful, and good or bad, among other labels. Because we feel pressured into fitting into the "right box," we tend to place a significant value on what others might think of us. We ride on the saying that "perception is reality," and then we adjust ourselves accordingly to be perceived in the "right" way. We minimize our internal values and focus on external ones.

Since a portion of my pathfinding business revolves around branding and brand development, I understand at a high level how perception affects opportunities. That means I also appreciate and understand the reflex to create a false journey to achieve various sensations in order to keep those perceptions alive. However, as I have learned in my own life, that is the easy way out and ultimately not very rewarding.

The interesting thing about expectations is that sometimes they are low. Some people (and some groups of people) don't have high expectations placed on them. And just like everyone else, they will—even subconsciously—try to honor those expectations. The effects of low expectations are just as debilitating as high expectations, and in some cases, even more so. Along our pathway to a more authentic life, we must learn to hold ourselves accountable to our own core values, ignoring the expectations of others to become anyone other than who we are.

Our truth eventually makes its way to the surface. It begins as a slight murmur of unhappiness that ultimately rages like the spiritual version of cardiac arrest. It impedes our creativity, our mental well-being, our purpose, our journey, and sometimes even our physical health. Initially, the slight murmurs can be handled with therapy and humor and by telling ourselves, and others, that we're OK. Sometimes we cope by overusing alcohol or medications; sometimes we attempt even more harmful tactics. Unfortunately, many people, regardless of wealth or fame, have truths that surface and lead them to a place where they attempt to take their own lives and/or the lives of others. Sadly, some are successful.

Some of those in the LOMB take notice of where they are and set their course for truth—despite what others may think. These people usually fare better on the other side because they have found their truth, and have become what I call LYTES (Live-Your-Truth-Experience Soldiers). They are fighting for truth despite being judged for refusing to conform.

So how do we end up in the LOMB? We are hand-delivered there by expectations without communication or consideration. From the moment we are born, expectations are placed upon us. When we come out of the womb, we're expected to cry and pee before we leave the hospital, not to mention arrive as a "beautiful" baby. When we are toddlers, we are expected to walk and use a toilet by a certain time. By the time we start school, the expectations start to run rampant. Read— fast! Be mannered—always! Clean your room—now! Study—hard! Play sports—well! Go to college—a good one! Get a job—a well-paying one! Stay thin—it's better. Get married—it's stable. Have children—it's fulfilling. Wear nice clothes—be accepted. Be famous—and get attention. I could keep going, and I'm sure you could continue this list with your own experiences and understanding of society pressures as well. This is how the course is set. The people who place the initial expectations upon us are usually well intentioned; they are often still living in the LOMB themselves, and they see no other way. It's what they know.

Maybe we are *also* holding other people accountable for playing a role in our lives or providing us with something for which they are unaware. We should all take time to pause and think about this at regular intervals. It is so easy for us to slip into these patterns. Awareness is the key for us to avoid unreasonable expectations on friends and family. We don't want them to do it to us, and we must be careful not to do it to them, too. We are striving to live a more authentic life. Let's not hold onto uncommunicated expectations that have not been agreed upon. This is not living true.

* * *

Sprinkling Pepper

While some expectations are necessary, they can also be very dangerous, especially if the person on the receiving end has no clue what those expectations are. On one hand, expectations provide some level of standard for what should take place in a given situation. On the other hand, they should be clearly established and communicated to ensure that the person who is being expected to live up to them can and wants to comply. Otherwise, it is a setup for failure, creating a false journey to sensations. When people expect us to behave in a certain way and we don't, they may be disappointed, surprised, or even angry. We see this daily with notable personalities who are demonized when something they did or didn't do fails to meet public expectations. Working with some of these personalities, I've come to realize that many of them have no idea what these expectations are, despite what we believe.

* * *

Some would argue that notable people should know what is expected of them because they've seen the journey played out before. But just imagine, for a moment, when you were a young person, hanging out with your friends, freely expressing yourself when you felt like it, and getting in trouble for mischievous behavior. Then you grew up.

Imagine having those free expressions of your youth placed in print and posted on the internet for everyone to read and comment upon with impunity. Imagine gaining ten pounds over the holiday season (as many of us are prone to do) and having pictures of you with the extra pounds and critical captions about it all over the Internet. Imagine getting a chance to finally close your eyes for just a few minutes at the airport after working seven straight sixteen-hour days only to be awakened by someone you don't know (a fan). If you have a slight attitude about being awakened, you are negatively labeled for not being more accommodating to a request for an autograph. Can you imagine having those kinds of expectations to perform placed on you? The price of fame is far higher than anyone can reasonably be expected to pay.

Even if you're not as famous as the personalities I'm speaking of, I would venture to say that people still expect many things of you. Some expectations you are aware of, and others you are not. These are the very expectations that launch so many of us into the LOMB. We try to live up to them while neither consulting our value system nor even understanding why we are trying to please these people who have placed these expectations upon us.

Have you ever had a friend, a coworker, a manager, a family member, or someone else express disappointment in something you did or didn't do—and you were unaware that the expectation even existed? Maybe you found out because your co-worker was a little cold and distant, or maybe your friend simply commenced to lay you out about it. Either way, your first reaction may have been surprise and then anger. How dare someone hold you accountable for something you didn't even know about or agree to? That's like having someone sue you for not performing professional services without ever hiring you directly.

We can expect our friends, family, and other community members to tell us when they have expectations for us, but that still does not confer upon us an obligation to comply. With the communication of expectations should come a review of our true values. This review will allow us to determine if the expectations are appropriate for us and if we will choose to live up to them.

We all have a choice in the matter as to whether we can oblige—a choice that shouldn't exist with a label but rather an understanding. Regardless of others' expectations, we have to set our own course to our truth based on our own personal values—*no matter* what others may think. Our life's fulfillment is at stake. Not Oprah's. Not Dr. Phil's. Ours. We get one shot at this. We can't waste it on regretting our past.

Once you are clear about your own core values, then you can move forward and align them with the people, places, and experiences that can help you to live your truth. This will cut down on your disappointments and on the time you spend trying to convert people to your way of thinking.

* * *

Sprinkling Pepper

Don't compare yourself to the "norm" or other people's value systems. Your gifts and truths are unique to you, and you need them all so you can take full advantage of this human experience. This is not to lead to complete individualism; this is to lead you to your own truth so you can affect the world in the way you are meant to. Otherwise, you're not getting access to all of your wonderful flavors that we all need to make this world a melting pot of stew that is more delicious. We want to make sure we add *all* the spices, especially the pepper, so we'll be sure to sneeze…in truth!

* * *

As I noted earlier, there are many situations where expectations are warranted and needed. I'm not suggesting that we give them up completely. We expect parents to love us, significant others to be faithful, and our siblings to have our back. When we find these basic expectations are not being met, this is a good sign that we need to re-evaluate our situation and see what we can do about it.

Here are a few other examples to further illustrate this notion of expectations. If you are perceived to have an abundance of wealth, you may be expected to give people money based on the perception that you have it to give. If you have achieved some level of success, then people expect you to maintain it. If you produced great grades in school, you are expected to land a great job. But the expectations can be even more broad and have little to do with us as individuals: If you are black, you are expected to speak some form of slang. If you are Asian, you are expected to be good at math. If you are white, you are expected to have little understanding of diversity issues. The problem here is that all of these expectations are based on what we perceive without looking any deeper than the surface. We don't actually have enough information to arrive at these expectations or to place these labels on these individuals or entire groups.

Mostly, we have the media and our small sampling of experiences to use as a reference. Sometimes those are all we use to go ahead and label everyone in a group, but that's taking the easy road, and it's incorrect. Without any understanding of a person's values, we really have no understanding of their truths. Along the same vein, we often adopt these expectations from society—how we should act and behave—without consulting our own value systems. That's the setup! That is why these expectations last from generation to generation and why it is so important to examine our *own* truths, which will hopefully keep us from labeling others.

We create expectations for each other based upon what *we* want rather than on each person's truth and what that individual is willing and able to do. This is where communication comes in. Yes, despite the rise of the Internet, social media, and texting, we still have to communicate with each other. For instance, we may fall in love with someone and develop expectations around who we want that person to be in our life. What we do from there is the determining factor of the success or failure of the relationship. At this point, we have options. We can each communicate our truth and values, allowing the other person to acknowledge them and determine if they are acceptable, or we can move forward with our unspoken expectations and hope that it all works out.

In relationships, both people should communicate their expectations as well as they can within their own truth. Otherwise, being in that relationship is like randomly jumping off a cliff, hoping to find water to break the fall. It's a much bigger gamble. If communicating and defining terms do not occur in the relationship, it is akin to two people attempting to travel the world together but refusing to discuss where they are going. They may eventually have to part ways if they are not traveling the same way; even if they are headed to the same destination. The Bible asks, "Do two walk together unless they have agreed to do so?"[3] The truth is that they don't. They *can't*.

Aligning our values and expectations with each other ensures that we *will* have water below to break the fall. If

---

3 Amos 3:3

we don't do this, then our significant other may continue to live our truth while sacrificing his or her own truth and will either become resentful or live unfulfilled (e.g., the martyr). Of course, the truth will eventually reveal itself and cause turmoil in the relationship. You have heard of oil rising to the top; when the infatuation stage is over, truth will rise to the top.

Real estate in the LOMB is very expensive. In the long run, the price is time, fulfillment, and happiness. Please note that this dynamic plays out in all kinds of relationships, such as employee-to-employer, friend-to-friend, parent-to-child, teacher-to-student, and so on.

Interestingly enough, some people *refuse* to accept any expectations placed on them because they don't like the sensations they cause. The sensation of *pressure*, to name one. They continue to underperform so that expectations remain either low or nonexistent. I believe many of us have had the experience of someone we live with claiming to have "cleaned" the bathroom, but then we find the toilet, floor and sink are still dirty, or a spouse promising to pick up the groceries but then "forgetting" so many items that we still have to go out and do the job ourselves. When it happens on a regular basis, it seems as if the goal here is to keep the expectations low, so maybe we won't ask for help again. One of my dearest friends calls it "being afraid of the sunshine." I say, "Bask in the light that is within your truth and shine."

This kind of low-expectation seeking plays out every day in various areas of people's lives. Some don't ever exceed expectations at work because they fear being expected to do more and that they will not be able to live up to the new expectations. They fear the sensation of *failing*. In relationships, it shows up the same way. Fear of success sometimes comes from the fear of failure. Perfection is not an attainable human goal. The only way we progress is through failing and learning, thus the expectation of perfection is a set up for failure anyway.

While the strategy of low-expectation seeking is outside my personal experience, I do understand how it happens. It can start gradually—often as a self-defense mechanism—and grow in frequency as it does work to keep people at a safe distance. However, as you examine your core values and the truth for your life, you will find that this existence is not enough for you. If you've started out with people not expecting much of you, it may be more difficult for you to turn things around. The problem with this is that because people don't expect much from you, they don't count on you for much either, so you have few chances to turn their opinions around. The impact of this is far reaching and can extend to missed opportunities to grow, which means you might never fully realize your true purpose or potential. When you are on this route, you are excluded from many awesome emotional sensations. The key to avoid missing out on authentic and desired emotional sensations is to identify your values, have some fun, and live true. It is okay if you fall down along the way. Get back up and keep going!

It is never too late for us to free ourselves from the LOMB. We can all experience living free in the LOAT, where our lives can be fully appreciated, our values can be stabilized, our truths can be realized, and our life's courses can be set for awesome sensations that make us—and the world we live in—better.

As a person who once firmly lived in and advocated for the LOMB, I am acutely aware of how easy it is to live there in some or all areas of your life. The point of recognizing where you are in your journey is not to judge it, but to live it—with your eyes wide open. Based on the things you truly value, you may learn that the journey you're on is right on target. Not every person buys expensive cars or lives in certain neighborhoods to appease external expectations. Many do so because these choices fully align with their value systems and their authentic lives. I'm just suggesting that we should examine our motivations to be sure.

* * *

Sprinkling Pepper
Why do people close their eyes when they're about to experience that drop on a roller coaster or bungee jump, or while watching a suspenseful part in a movie? Because they don't want to see what's coming next. Similarly,

people who go through life not looking will not see what's coming. Thus, they end up taking or responding to what life dishes out instead of being prepared to choose where life might take them.

* * *

As you let go of others' expectations of you and begin to live your own values, you will find yourself welcomed to the LYTE (Live-Your-Truth Experience). You can become an ambassador of truth, fighting against the false journey to your sensations. Live your truth!

* * *

Chapter 3 Reflections

- If you're in the LOMB, you're not alone.

- Understand the expectations people in your life have of you.

- Be clear about the expectations you have of others and don't assume.

- Don't be afraid of the sunshine; live in the expectations you have of yourself.

- Be prepared to respond to life by knowing what you expect from it.

~ 4 ~

THE SENSATION SELECTION

Developing Our Preferences

I grew up in the city of Philadelphia in a place called Mount Airy with my mother and younger sister. My neighborhood was filled with children of varying backgrounds: black, white, Asian, and Latino. Like most communities, expectations were set for every child who lived in our neighborhood. These expectations were set by both the adults and the other children. For instance, our parents expected us to be respectful of other adults, to get high grades in school, and to be inside before the streetlights came on (until a certain age). Our friends expected us to join group games, and to do all of the things that little girls and boys were "supposed to do." I had the additional expectation to be able to spiral a football. My neighbor, Sean, taught me and made sure I practiced. He liked to tease some of the guys in the neighborhood by telling them he knew a girl who could throw better than they could. I must say that the sensations of *accomplishment* and *recognition* felt fantastic, even though they are not my preferred sensations.

Although I was reserved early in life, I made friends very easily and did very well in school. I was particularly good at math and was, for the most part, a pleasant child who followed the rules and didn't cause much trouble. I was expected to be this way—whether because I was a firstborn or simply because those were the natural expectations for a child in my family and community—and I strove to live up to those expectations. Except for the occasional spanking—given for

mouthing off or getting caught sneaking out to a party—
I didn't give my mother much trouble. My younger sister,
Tiffany, on the other hand, was another story. She seemed
to be motivated more by the sensation of *adventure* than by
the sensation of *approval* from adults.

* * *

Sprinkling Pepper
**Take a minute to think about who you were while
growing up: What kinds of things did you like? How
would people have described you? Remember what made
you feel special or happy. Was it praise, achievement,
recognition, affection, or some other thing? Keep these
questions on the radar for the value-identification exercise at the end of this book.**

* * *

My mother taught us many amazing lessons that continue to serve me well. One of them was "image is everything," which actually turned out to be a pretty amazing
lesson. However, this mantra also fit neatly into the LOMB.
The "image is everything" lesson was originally meant to
teach me to apply care to the condition of my homework
and my personal appearance. It was meant to encourage me
to attend to my posture, my clothes, my hair, my room,
my homework, and any other aspect of myself that was expected to be neat and well-cared for. This attention to image
resulted in the application of labels of "well-put together,"
"attractive," etc. which created a sensation of recognition.

While it was not a desired sensation, it felt awesome. What things "appeared to be" became very important to me. I remember writing my homework over many times to ensure it was perfectly neat so I could get recognition from my teachers and peers. It worked.

As part of my dedication to my mother's lesson about image, I began to refuse to be seen in the same article of clothing more than once a week because I didn't want people to know that I didn't have a lot of clothes. My mother was beside herself once when she asked me to go pick up my sister from the hair salon where she worked as a shampoo girl. I said I couldn't because I'd already worn the top I had on earlier in the week, and I didn't want anyone to see me wearing it again. As you can imagine, my mother gave me "the look," and I went inside to get my sister, repeat shirt and all. The story gives me the giggles when I think about it now, but at the time, I wasn't happy about it at all!

Because I became good with numbers in high school, most adults in my life expected that I would go to college and major in finance or some math-related subject. Majoring in finance would make my mother and other adults proud. Their logic was that since I had a natural affinity for math, finance would land me a "great" job in a "stable" profession. So, without thinking to check into what a job "in finance" would actually entail day to day and how it aligned with my personal protocol, I ventured off to the lovely campus of Hampton University to study math and finance.

My first year was fantastic! I missed my mother terribly at first, but other than that, life was grand. Most of the classes were not in my major, and I ended up taking lots of electives. I enjoyed a relatively good year academically. My second year was a little tougher. That was the year I pledged Delta Sigma Theta, which was very time consuming. Some of the young women pledging to our sorority that year continued to find time to study. Some of us had a more difficult time managing our pledge duties, studies, and sleep. When I say some, I certainly am including myself.

At Hampton, both worlds of the Land of Make-Believe (LOMB) and the Land of Authenticity and Truth (LOAT) were present. It was a time for exploring our truths and finding out who we were. Over time, many of us began to or continued to crave all kinds of emotional sensations like feeling *loved, accepted, acknowledged, considered, and respected.* And because we were transitioning into adulthood, we also experienced sensations like *disappointment, envy, jealousy,* and *heartbreak.* The whole experience was amazing! I ultimately found my balance and graduated with a degree in finance and accounting. I had fulfilled a sensation of *pleasing.*

My first job was as a health care benefits analyst with a major health insurance company. I made a lot of money in overtime, but I was not fulfilled. At the time, I didn't even think it was important to be fulfilled. I was enjoying the sensations of *having.* I had no interest in moving out of my professional LOMB.

Judging by my own standards, I can say that my early twenties were nothing short of phenomenal. I was hanging tight on the entertainment scene with one of my dearest friends, Mo Ivory, and we were "livin' *la vida loca*." We were traveling to Martha's Vineyard on Cape Cod and attending record-release parties, movie premieres, celebrity birthday bashes, NBA all-star weekends, and more. My friend Robyn, who was a fellow shopaholic, would assist me in selecting the many styles I donned in the LOMB. I call this the LOMB because I couldn't really afford the clothes I was buying to maintain my image. I was chasing the "good" labels.

The LOMB in the aesthetic department was in full effect, and we were fully immersed in it. All that mattered was what it looked like. Strangely enough, while it may have seemed tempting to do so, I was not in jeopardy of joining the entertainment industry's LOMB, which was a value compromise on another level, or trading in my values for theirs. From television appearances to the paparazzi to the tabloids, the expectation to be what society expected was great. I saw the excitement in their lives, but I also saw the sacrifices they had to make in order to maintain their places in the LOMB. The sacrifices they had to make to their own values in order to live up to others' expectations seemed much greater and more invasive to me than the sacrifices I made in my own LOMB. No matter how glamorous the atmosphere looked, I was going back to my corporate job, my own LOMB.

Unfortunately, the murmurs of unfulfillment at my corporate job were becoming a steady, low hum. I didn't recognize it then, but I was beginning to suffer from the value compromise; the craving for the good labels was beginning to supersede my own value system. One of the things I have often been fully aware of as valuable to me is *purpose*, but the sensations of *recognition* and *having* continued to prevail. Without knowledge of sensation chasing, you are prone to go off the rails in hot pursuit of them.

I tried other jobs but, with the exception of a stint I did in human resources, stayed in finance-related roles, and for many years, I made more money than I ever expected. In each position, from auditor to accounting management, one thing was evident: I eventually strongly disliked my job, but I couldn't understand why. I still liked math, so what was the problem? I really needed a truth moment.

* * *

Sprinkling Pepper
Understanding when we're in the zone professionally is a great first step to identifying our truth in our professional purpose. The zone is the place where we could do or talk about a certain thing all day. If we know we are going to wake up and be able to do this thing, we may have trouble sleeping the night before because we're so excited about it. People call us to do this thing. We're good at it, and while we're doing it, we don't need as

much sleep or food. It incorporates our truth at its most basic place.

* * *

What I came to realize after years in finance was that it didn't incorporate enough of my value elements for me to thrive. For the first time, I realized that being good at something did not necessarily mean that I should do it for a living. The elements I needed professionally have always included things like strategizing, consideration, problem solving, autonomy, creativity, and variety; I also craved lots of people interaction, big picture thinking, and communication. These things were just not the predominant features of a career in finance. So I had my big "aha!" moment, but what could I do about it?

When this revelation came, I was a married twenty-something with a son and the financial responsibilities that came with living an upper middle-class life. I was working—in finance—at a fitness-apparel company and running my pathfinding company part-time. Onlookers might have said my life was great, some may have even been a little envious, but I was at a crossroads.

Right in the middle of all my external success and internal restlessness, I received a call from one of my favorite mentors and friends; she had a lead for a job with a commercial real estate firm. Despite being settled into the LOMB at my current company, she advised me to take the interview. She believed that, at a minimum, I should hear the company out. I followed her advice and took the interview. To my delight, they spoke my language of autonomy and problem solving, all within an entrepreneurial atmosphere. I felt a surge of the sensation of *thriving*. Sensations can be euphoric in the moment. I was in and ready to start!

I gave two weeks' notice to the apparel company, packed my desk, said my good-byes, and prepared to travel to the big city. I started as the Operations Manager for the New England area of this commercial real estate firm—in the dead of winter in downtown Boston. It was February, and I was three months' pregnant with my second son.

By the time my second son was born, that sense of professional unfulfillment was creeping in. Although I was no longer in the fitness apparel industry and the atmosphere was much more entrepreneurial, finance was still a significant part of the job. They had been very clear about that in the interview, but the new elements of this job that were presented rang out more loudly.

It's easy to get caught up in the new and sensational and forget to take a moment to assess the opportunity against your values. The job was full of things to do: budgets, HR, and paperwork, paperwork, paperwork. I had reviews to write, escrow accounts to open, budgets to forecast, administrative assistants to manage, checks to sign, and more. I certainly did not have a shortage of things to do. The pay was more than sufficient, and I was always busy. I was also bored stiff. The work was plentiful, but it just wasn't interesting enough to me.

As I became increasingly frustrated with the lack of mental stimulation in my commercial real estate job, I began to notice the brokers in the firm—the hustle, the camaraderie, the presentations, and the sweet checks they received. Along the way, I have been very clear about my desire to gain a certain level of wealth to take care of my family and assist others with their dreams. Brokerage seemed like a great way to achieve those goals. So I inquired about a position in brokerage by having a discussion with the head of the Downtown Team. He was a person who had always been straight with me, whether I wanted to hear it or not. And this time was no exception.

He was very honest about the nuances of brokerage and the challenges he thought I might face—both as a newbie and as woman of color in Greater Boston. Because being a "hard worker" is a label you definitely want in commercial real estate, I went into label-chasing mode and worked through my entire maternity leave to get that label before my job change. A value compromise for sure.

I also hung out with the brokers and learned more about what was required to do the job. Foremost were people skills. Check. Problem solving. Check. Strategizing.

Check. Networking. Check. Negotiating. Check. I felt that surge of new purpose! I was in again! I hired someone to replace me as operations manager, and I was headed into brokerage.

As one of my friends and mentors has so lovingly pointed out, when my laser is focused on something, I make it happen. I studied for the real estate exam, passed it, and became a broker at the same firm where I had been the operations manager. Fanfare ensued. Once I got the job, I made the front page of the business section of *The Boston Globe* newspaper because I was the first black broker for the New England area of this real estate firm and also the first black female broker for any major commercial real estate firm in Massachusetts. This added an unexpected level of pressure to my new endeavor. I was humbled and excited, but most of all, I wanted to be successful in my new role. I will admit that my desire for success was initially based on the expectations that came from onlookers, the media, brokers, and of course, me. I didn't realize it at the time, but I had traded one LOMB for another.

My first challenge was addressing the need for an appropriate network to get the job done. I'd been in Boston for nine years, and I knew a lot of people, but most of them were not in the positions I needed to get these deals done. One's success in commercial real estate is heavily built on social relationships, and Bostonians are very connected to one another from way back. It takes a long time to move into the social/non business related realm. And since I wasn't from the area, it was a tougher process to break into the "in the know" of the Boston network. I love a good challenge, especially in the area of getting to know people, but it was also another setup for living in the LOMB. When your goal is to "fit in," you can feel the need to comply with some form of conformity and value compromise.

I have learned now to seek acceptance in circles that align with my values as opposed to "fitting in" with the group with the higher perceived status. I can bring myself—quirks and all—with my grounded abilities and my well-intentioned heart, and rather than create a facade that is situated perfectly for a particular group, I can let people decide if they can accept me and my truth.

The second challenge was that none of the other brokers looked like me. I wasn't afraid that people would refuse to hire me because I was a woman of color; I was concerned that they would assume I didn't know the "right" people, especially since deals were made based primarily on *whom* you knew and *who* knew you. I knew this would be a great challenge, and I was excited to see what I could do!

I hit the ground running by sending out personal handwritten notes to almost everyone I knew in business in Boston. Within three months, I had a wonderful fish on the line. It came in the form of a former employer with whom I had maintained a great relationship.

* * *

Sprinkling Pepper
Building authentic relationships is critical to, not only our professional success, but also our personal development. Relationships offer a variety of benefits that are not all the same. Nurture them.

* * *

The company, while small, was high profile, and many people wanted to know how I knew such a contact. Remember, because I was an "outsider," the assumption was that my contacts were limited. Sometimes being underestimated is just the thing you need to push yourself even harder. For some, it triggers the sensation of *proving*. This may not be the best sensation to strive for since you can easily lose focus when your motivation is external, but it certainly worked for me in this situation, at least temporarily. My competitive spirit took charge and launched me straight into the LOMB, where the feelings associated with success through someone else's eyes became too important.

Generally speaking, things were good during this phase of my life. I was married to a wonderful man, we lived in a beautiful home, and I was living happily in the LOMB. I was the mother of two amazing little boys, I had incredible friends, went on relaxing vacations to great places, performed board service, worked in the community, and now I had a challenging job with all the elements I thought I needed to thrive.

Look at all those labels in the preceding paragraph: *good, wonderful, beautiful, amazing, incredible,* and *great.* I take a moment to point this out because we chase labels in the LOMB, not truth. Who wouldn't want these labels, however subjective they may be?

Things changed over the next several years, especially as my truth began to further rise to the surface at work and at home. My marriage was on the rocks, and I was growing tired of the brokerage environment. While my position in brokerage called for great people skills as well as abilities with problem solving, strategizing, networking, negotiating, and a high level of autonomy—many of my professional values—I realized I wasn't at all interested in the subject matter. In addition, the level of closed-mindedness that I found in the atmosphere was not aligned with my core values.

Boom! It was as if a bomb detonated in my life. The financial crisis hit, my marriage was failing, and I was working in an industry that was experiencing an extreme amount of turmoil. I felt panicked and needed a minute to figure out how I got on such unstable ground, but life kept moving. People continued to congratulate me for the job I was doing in brokerage and for being able to handle all the pressures of being the "only" in a white, male-dominated field. Some continued to comment on how beautiful my family was and how lucky I must have felt. I actually did feel fortunate to have a great family, but I still felt like I was drowning.

Remember all the *Boston Globe* fanfare I mentioned? Well, the sensation of *pride* was at play, as was the pressure to prove I could do the job and be successfully married. It was the sensation of *succeeding*, despite the cost to truth. I sat on various panels, and they asked me questions such as, "How do you keep it all together with everything you have going on?" How could I possibly tell them it wasn't real, that they shouldn't look at me with such envy, and that I was living in the LOMB? No matter how much I wanted out, I couldn't bear the embarrassment of people knowing I wasn't living my truth. I mean, I had just figured it out myself. I was still trying to hang on to the sensation of *pride*.

I tried to focus on the positive aspects of my life. Although I knew I was not living my truth, I was also not living in an endless, horrible stream of facades and phoniness: I had two amazing children, and even though our marriage was failing, their father remained present and engaged in their lives. I had supportive friends, phenomenal mentors, a caring extended family, resources, and lots of laughs. However, I couldn't be the best "me" that I was called to be in the life I'd created. Big parts of my life were not being lived in my complete truth, and this ultimately affected everything else. After a while, the facade made it feel as if *everything* was a lie. I got confused as it became hard to tell the difference between the LOMB and the LOAT.

I was trying to put my game face on at home, but I was making everyone in my house miserable. I was the one living in the LOMB; they were being true to the person they believed me to be. I needed to do something to get back to the LOAT. Unfortunately, I knew the first step was to leave my marriage. While my then husband and I had had a great relationship for many years, I had been unaware of my truth. Once I understood it, I struggled to communicate my truth while we were married. That is not a foundation for a sustainable marriage.

My husband was frustrated, and so was I, but it was very difficult to find a way to tell him how bad it was. He hadn't done anything wrong: He was a good person and a wonderful father. It was very hard to tell him that the things I thought I wanted were not all true to my core values. The life we had created was safe and routine, but it had so many boundaries that I felt trapped and panicked.

One thing I learned about myself during this time was that when I am faced with no options, I create new options to achieve my goals. It's part of who I am. Eventually, I broke the news to my then-husband. Along with extreme sadness came the sensation of *relief.* I was going to be free from that place in the LOMB.

I did not like being the cause of so much pain in my family, and I felt very guilty for making them go through this process to help me reach my LOAT. I felt selfish for needing more than our life provided. And it pained me deeply that my family was going to be apart.

I also felt conflicted spiritually. After all, the Bible says, and I quote, "I hate divorce…"[4] This verse repeated itself in my heart over and again and caused me great pain. I wanted to believe God still loved me dearly throughout my divorce and that my relationship with him could never be compromised. I knew that his love was great enough to overcome all my shortcomings, but truly internalizing this truth took some time. Once I did, my spirit was freed from my perceived bondage, and I was rejuvenated.

After my husband, the most difficult person to tell was my mother. Then I had to tell everyone else: my extended family, my friends, and my co-workers. Most people were saddened to hear the news, and some tried to talk me out of the divorce.

Throughout the process, people were in disbelief, and some people passed judgment on me for my decisions. I knew that I was in pursuit of my truth and core values, despite the many positive and temporary emotional sensations I was experiencing. And through it all, I prayed a lot. I held on to the belief that tough times are temporary.

* * *

---

4 Malachi 2:16

Chapter 4 Reflections

- It is perfectly normal in the world we live in to struggle to find our values.

- We mustn't ignore our spirit when it tells us we're on the wrong path.

- Label chasing is prevalent in our society; we're not alone.

- Chasing labels will not bring us happiness. We must lock into our values and stick with them.

~ 5 ~

SENSATION SATISFYING

Giving In

My dad left our family when I was just five years old and my sister was two. He left to find his own truth in dealing with his mental issues. People often ask me if I am angry about this, and I can honestly say that I am not. I never was. My dad suffered from schizophrenia, and he thought our lives would be easier without him. I can only imagine how difficult it must have been for him to make that incredibly unselfish decision for his family. In my eyes, he had a legitimate reason, but even if he had simply decided that he just didn't want to be tied down to a family, I would still not be upset with him for leaving. I would rather he had gone on to live his truth than to stay and be miserable.

My mother raised us alone, and she did an amazing job, I might add. We laughed a lot while growing up. No matter what we were facing, we always had laughter. My mother has a way of seeing the bright side of everything. I am forever grateful that she passed that optimism along to my sister and me. I never saw her ask for help. She just did what needed to be done and always rose to the occasion. She also passed this value down to me. This truth of not asking for help has served me well in certain aspects of my business and not so well in romance.

One month before I was going to move out of the house, I drove to Philly to visit my mother and tell her about my pending divorce. I dreaded telling her so much that I waited until just before it was time for me to get on the road back to Boston to break the news to her.

My mother was very calm, asked if I was sure, and said she was saddened by it. She also wanted to know if my then-husband and the boys were doing OK. Most importantly, she said she understood and wanted me to be happy.

It is so interesting how many people looked at my circumstances—independent of knowing me personally—and thought I was crazy for the decision I was making. Perhaps by their definition of crazy I may have been, but that would be their truth. Their truth cannot define mine. Their truth cannot define yours. We can each only define our own truths, and we can make a profound impact on this world by respecting each other's truths.

Since I was the one who was redefining my truth, my husband and I agreed that I would leave the house, and we would split the boys' time fifty-fifty. When I got to an emotionally comfortable place, I began to address the next item on the list: my job. This was another area in my LOMB (Land of Make-Believe) where I wasn't being true to myself. Commercial real estate brokerage was definitely a high-profile job, especially because at the time I was still the only black woman doing it. I met amazing people, had challenging assignments, and learned something new every day. However, the overall environment was not aligned with who I was and what I wanted to stand for. Finding another truth while going through a divorce was both an outgrowth and an enhancement of the sensation of freedom.

An element of complete truth in my brokerage position came in the form of my mentor, the head of the Downtown team in my commercial real estate firm, whom I mentioned earlier. He provided much-needed guidance and strong doses of "life is tough, but with hard work you can get through it" messages that always seemed to take the pressure off. His support gave me the gift of the sensation of *understanding*, and knowing that he understood my situation gave me the peace I needed to move forward in my life.

During this time, life *was* tough, both emotionally and financially. The commercial real estate environment doesn't suffer fools, which was actually one of the things I really liked about it, and it contributed greatly to the success I have experienced in my other ventures. Since I don't enjoy a lot of drama in business environments, it was perfect. I liked most of the people I worked with, and we had no shortage of laughs; however, when it was time to work, we got down to business. In spite of my marriage and my deteriorating financial situation, I went to work and worked hard every day. I was still living solidly in the LOMB because I didn't think I could tell anyone what I was going through. After all, the expectation was, "Monica is doing great" and "she can handle it."

Another thing I learned during my transition from the LOMB is that demons haunt you the most when you keep them a secret. The fear of being found out can be debilitating. That is the ultimate gold standard for living in the LOMB. So I decided to share my home and financial situations with a few key people in my personal and professional circles. This didn't bring resolution to my problems, but it sure helped me to sleep better at night. In contrast to the people in my outer circle in whom I initially confided, the people in my inner circle were extremely supportive, even if they just listened. When I let go of those secrets, I experienced a wonderful sensation of *freedom*. This was a very important lesson in my transition. Image isn't *always* everything. As a matter of fact, recognizing the truth that there is more to every situation than what we perceive is just the beginning of exploration.

Money was still tight, to say the least; the real estate market continued to tank, but life continued to have some wonderful elements to it. That June, around the same time that my finances were falling apart, I was finishing up a wonderful social justice leadership program called LeadBoston. As the final task, we were asked to write letters to ourselves that would be mailed back to us in January. We were to reflect on our year in the program and then write down what we thought the future would look like for us. Although my situation at that time looked grim, I had many positive qualities in my life to keep me looking forward to the future: my incredible mother, guiding mentors, supportive friends, continual reasons to laugh, and my faith in God kept me intact.

God has always been evidently present in my life, both loudly and quietly; even during this dark time in my life, I believed he was still present. Whether it was by my own missteps or a lesson he had for me, I always believed the Bible verse that says, "And we know that in all things God works for the good of those who love him, [and] have been called according to his purpose."[5] I may have had to suffer a big hit to my pride, but I was coming out on the other side, intact and in my truth. I had to.

* * *

Sprinkling Pepper
Life will throw a few curveballs, regardless of your faith, financial status, family situation, or experiences. They may come in the form of a loved one dying, a family breakup, a loss of resources, health issues, abandonment by someone you love, or the realization that you've not lived your truth. In those moments, the important thing to remember is the truth of the moment. You choose how to respond in and to the moment. Let victory be your choice.

* * *

Nearly a year after I moved out of the family home, I still carried a lot of guilt for not being able to stay in the

---

5 Rom. 8:28

marriage. Still, the boys had adjusted, and my ex and I were working well together as co-parents. We were still a family in our own way, and we were all learning how to live our lives in my new truth.

Financially, things had gotten worse, but God came through as always. Just when I needed it most, I closed a real estate deal that put me in a much better financial position to move forward. You can imagine how I gave God resounding thanks and praise! Around this same time, a longtime mentor reached out to me and asked if I would like to meet him for dinner while he was in town.

We met at Boston's Grille 23 on a cold fall night and had a great time catching up. He told me about his nuptials and the newest member of his family, who was then five; I told him about my pending divorce, my job in real estate, and my growing pathfinding company. I was most enthusiastic about discussing my pathfinding company. I could talk about it all day. He must have felt the passion that I had for it because by the end of dinner, he asked me to give him a number—a dollar figure—of how much I thought it would take for me to run my company full-time! I was excited, speechless, and so grateful for the affirmation. I knew that this offer could not be taken lightly, so that Friday, I treated myself to a nice dinner, locked myself in my home, and developed a business plan to make my part-time brand company a full-time venture.

Monday morning I e-mailed him and sent a copy of that plan via FedEx. The wait was on but not for long.

The following Saturday, while visiting with my friend Patrice, I received a text message saying, "I made a decision to fund your business."

I could not believe my eyes. What did that text just say? So I read it again.

"I made a decision to fund your business." Yes, that's what it said.

I sat in silence for a moment and then looked up at Patrice, and with tears in my eyes, I said, "Guess what, girl?"

She was in awe and so happy for me.

I worshipped God as the tears came flowing from my eyes. They came for the struggle of the last few years. They came for the unwavering commitment I had to coming out of my unfulfilling circumstances. They came for the legacy I would leave my sons. They came for the joy of having some-one believe in my passion. They came because God was the tried and ultimate truth in my life. They came simply from gratitude. They came as I felt the power I gain from *believing*.

As you can imagine, I went to work the next day with a new pep in my step. I had so much to do to prepare for my departure. During this time, I had the pleasure of being reintroduced to Jeff Taylor, a brilliant entrepreneur, brand strategist extraordinaire, and founder of Monster.com, EONs, and Meetcha. We had coffee to catch up with each other. During the course of that conversation, he offered office space to me for my new business. He also vowed to make himself available to mentor me whenever I needed it.

What was going on here? An angel investor pops up out of nowhere, and then the founder of Monster.com—a brand guru—was going to mentor me? Seriously?

The clarity of my truth was starting to shine through. I had been looking for the right path for my truth, and a path had opened up for me.

I made plans, organized myself, and left the real estate job in January of 2010. I was in a good place. My truth was present and being revealed at lightning speed. The funny thing was that during this entire journey and after sharing my truths with others, people started sharing theirs with me. I heard countless stories from people about how they were compromising their truths for acceptance, other people compromised for the perception that all was well, and some for the hope of a reward promised by the same society that had suggested the values they were living by. These were not all unhappy and downtrodden people; they were simply people who could acknowledge the various areas where they had bought into the LOMB to achieve various sensations.

The people in my life who knew what I was going through at the time may have thought I was in denial because I wasn't falling apart during all the turmoil. It's important to understand your mode of operation and then not to compare it to others. To date, I haven't been one who usually falls apart in the midst of struggle or flies off the handle when angry. This doesn't mean that I don't have feelings or emotions; it just means that I'm more of a calm personality in certain situations. I've learned through this journey to authentic living that my go-to question in every instance is, "What can I do about it right now?" If I can do something to solve, rectify, or otherwise change the situation then I do it. If I can't, then I move on.

Now that you know my story and how I arrived here, let's begin your journey toward finding your awesome emotional sensations and ultimately your authentic life.

* * *

Chapter 5 Reflections

- Living your truth is fulfilling for you and others in your life.

- Your story is necessary.

- Building meaningful relationships is a mutually beneficial practice.

- You are not on this journey to truth alone.

- If people in your circles cannot handle your truth, remember that it is your truth, not theirs.

~ 6 ~

THE ORIGIN OF SENSATION

Why Are You Sneezing?

The Origin Of Sensation

Do you know what your values are? Or where they came from? These are not trick questions. They are ones that I thought I had the answers to for many years. I'm pretty sure they went something like, God, family, work, and they came from my family and community. That's what we're supposed to say, right? Obviously, some of us may have a slightly different list or have our items in a different order, but this basic list is often taught in various social groups— church, scouts, or the military, for instance—in America.

If you'd taken a deeper dive into my life in my twenties, you might have said that my values were: work, me, friends, God, and family. I worked all the time, and I played really hard with the money I made from work. Afterwards, I would have a moment of honesty, pray, and go to church to ask forgiveness for all that I had been doing that was not pleasing to God according to my religion. I also spent time with my family and friends, but not as much as I worked and played.

Values go even deeper than just how you spend your time. Values are actually what you live by; how you behave. For instance, if one of your values is excellence then it's probably something that you strive for in many areas, as well as what you expect from others. And when others don't live by it, it can be an irritant or a pet peeve. The same applies if you value consideration, which happens to be in my top five. You live that value in almost everything you do.

When others are inconsiderate, the value conflict causes a real problem for you.

So when I ask the question, do you know what your values are, I really mean do you have a full understanding of the code you live by? Do you know your personal protocol? Take a moment and think about it. You can use the exercise at the end of this book to assist you in discovering these values. It is important as you move forward in truth to know them. You will want to be open to the chance that you may not have full clarity around your core values yet. This is the case for many. When your values are clear, your purpose is easier to find, your emotional volatility is minimal, your self-confidence is at an all time high, and you have an amazing ability to identify truth and resist label chasing. We are going to talk a little bit more about values because values are the meat of this whole thing.

A value is a principle, standard, or quality considered worthwhile or desirable. The values we identify with will determine the choices we make aesthetically, relationally, spiritually, emotionally, financially, professionally, and parentally. We began developing our values when we were young. Some of them came from our core; others were suggested by external sources, such as family, media, and peers, to name a few.

Although we don't often consciously think of it, our values show up in some way each day. And, when we are unaware of them, they can influence our emotional state. Our values may include things like privacy, friendship, knowledge, consideration, efficiency, freedom, inclusion, image, and material possessions, to name a few. While values should ultimately be evident in the way we behave and the choices we make, we are usually too busy chasing our desired emotional sensations to define what is most important to us. And, without a clear set of values to live by, we end up utilizing the values that are both blatantly and subliminally suggested to us by our families or society. This is why so many of us look back, full of regret, and begin the search to try to figure out exactly who we are. The conversation has to be more deliberate, as does the identification of our values. It is critical to our freedom, our purpose, and our fulfillment.

The goal is to end up with a set of values we identify with, understand, and believe in our core. It takes a lot of self-examination to arrive at this place. Identifying our values will assist us greatly in knowing who we truly are and understanding the best and least regrettable path to our desired emotional sensations. In order to do this, we need to locate where we are currently. We can start by noticing our own behaviors. If we get irritated when people ask us if we fulfilled a promise, then we may value dependability or integrity. If we brag a lot about our accomplishments, then we may value recognition. If we become afraid when change happens, then stability may be one of our core values.

Be sure to take some time to complete the value-identification exercise at the end of the book. This will allow you to see your values in print, which can help you to understand your behaviors and how to respond authentically. What you believe affects the way you feel, and the way you feel affects what you do. The outcomes of your actions strengthen what you believe, either negatively or positively. It's a cycle.

Some of the things we use as indicators to show the world that we deserve the labels we seek are: "perfect" marriages, expensive clothes, fine cars, accomplished children, thin bodies, VIP access, fame, fortune, recognition, perfect images, great jobs, and more. We also use these things to create our desired emotional sensations. However, we must take a deeper dive to understand the value at the origin of the sensation; this will lead us to truth. In other words, getting to the root of our behavior, as well as our emotional triggers is the key to understanding ourselves.

The goal is to have our values at the core of our actions and not the desire for the labels. If you are unclear about your core values, your actions could be mistaken as being market value led—led by external sources—instead of core value led—led by internal sources. For instance, when you speak highly about your accomplishments, watch various news shows, ask lots of questions, or analyze information, you may be chasing the label of "smart" or simply living out your core value of knowledge. The goal is to let go of any label chasing and to simply adhere to the value. Know the difference.

If you became an entrepreneur, moved out of your parent's house early, refused to ask for help when needed, or divorced an overbearing spouse, you may be chasing the label of success, or it could be that independence is actually one of your core values. Again, the goal is to let go of any label chasing and to simply adhere to the value.

When respect is a core value, you might stop speaking to a friend who is regularly late for appointments with you, cut off a person who constantly makes you the butt of jokes, or report a coworker who makes passes at you. I'm sure you can guess what I'm going to say here. Stick to your values.

Health could be at the core of eating well, exercising, meditating, or practicing yoga. Excellence could be at the core of working hard, studying, or setting high standards. Truth could be at the core of exploring all avenues, asking questions, or challenging notions. Health, honesty, communication, consideration, and respect, among many others, are all values that cause emotional responses when they are in conflict with people or circumstances. Many of us can relate to this.

We run into trouble when we label our values either good or bad. This labeling system causes us to explain away or even deny our true core values and to take on those we see categorized as "good" or "desirable" labels in our society. For example, you may truly value experiences more than material possessions. However, the people in your work circles may value those who live in elaborate homes and drive expensive cars more highly than they value those with varied experiences. So if *acceptance* is a sensation you seek, then you may trade the experiences you truly want to have in order to purchase high-ticket material possessions and appease the folks at work. After years of this, your truth will cry out, and you will hear it. The sensation of *unfulfillment* is loud.

The important question to ask yourself when you're working toward a sensation is why. *Why do I want to feel this way, and what does it mean to me when I do?* It is equally important that you not judge your reason for wanting the sensation, but rather, take comfort in the fact that you are now aware of what you desire to feel. When you understand what brings you joy, anger, and sadness, when you learn what makes you feel filled with purpose, then you are less likely to live in the LOMB (Land of Make-Believe). The understanding that you gain gives you a foundational understanding of what makes you tick. This, in turn, will help you to resist the urge to chase sensations and labels and will assist you with your emotional well-being. Once you have identified your values, you can utilize these foundational truths to achieve the sensation directly instead of entering into the tidal wave of a propaganda-driven value system.

Try to remember a time when you did something for any reason other than that you really wanted to. For example, maybe you overrode your value of friendship first by sleeping with someone for the sensation of *love*. Maybe you drank too much with friends for the sensation of *acceptance* or took a job that didn't line up with your values for the sensation of *acknowledgement*. Perhaps you married a person who wasn't a fit with you for the sensation of *pleasing*, broke up with someone you really loved and wanted to be with for the sensation of *respect*, or had a baby when you weren't ready in order to experience the sensation of *love*. Maybe you gave up on a dream, didn't say, "I love you," or said no to a friend who asked for your help. Why did you do that? Were you denying a value for a sensation?

* * *

Sprinkling Pepper

Why we sneeze is just as important as what we're sneezing. Understanding *why* we desire to feel a certain emotional sensation is just as critical as *what* the desired sensation is. The journey to the sensations we seek defines who we are. It's how we will be remembered because it includes our behaviors and encompasses the ways in which we touch lives along our journey. For instance, if you are seeking to "sneeze" *acceptance* because you never felt good enough for your father, then you may want to examine this for a greater understanding. You may never be able to get the acceptance you are seeking from him, but you can stop holding other people accountable for making you feel accepted. That is living your truth.

* * *

73

Your whys may include comments such as "I don't like to be second-guessed" or "My father used to say he would be there and didn't show up" or "None of my teachers thought I would be successful" or "We were poor growing up" or many others. Our experiences, or lack thereof, sometimes lead us to place value on certain things we wouldn't otherwise care so much about. Delving into the whys will assist you in ridding yourself of the baggage you've collected from unresolved situations and allow you to live more true to yourself. Do not carry false truths into your future any longer.

At the end of this book, you can find an "Identifying Your Values Exercise." It is designed to help you determine what it is that you value generally and in the seven critical areas of your life (aesthetically, relationally, spiritually, emotionally, financially, professionally, and parentally). When you go through this exercise, take your time to go through it thoroughly.

Understanding these values will make the difference between living and existing, and between looking back on your life fondly or with regret. It will assist you in your search for purpose and in your quest for fulfillment.

* * *

Chapter 6 Reflections

- Identify your values for personal understanding.

- Use your value compass as a barometer for how successful your life is.

- Don't label the truth.

- Gain understanding of your desired sensations.

~ 7 ~

THE LOMB AND THE LOAT

Make Believe versus Truth

The Lomb And The Loat

Before we dive into a further exploration of our values and our quest for desired sensations, I would like to expound upon the Land of Make-Believe (LOMB)[6] and the Land of Authenticity and Truth (LOAT)[7]. These are both very present places of residence in our society. How closely we follow our Truth-Positioning System (TPS) will determine where we are on the spectrum between the LOMB and the LOAT. Our TPS, much like a GPS, allows us to pinpoint our location at any given time. By putting in our value coordinates and setting the "sensation destination," we can ensure that our TPS will lead us to authentic living.

In the LOMB, things are perceived to be a certain way, but with more information, we find out they may be something else. This applies to how we look at our lives and the lives of others. For instance, if you know a family that is always traveling to exotic and expensive locations for vacation, you may assume that they are wealthy and doing very well. That's a LOMB moment. Going on vacation to expensive places doesn't necessarily correlate to wealth or success. Another part of the LOMB creeps in when you develop sensations of *inadequacy* because you can't afford such vacations. That is an example of trying to take on the values of someone else without first locating yourself on your own TPS.

---

6   Pronounced to rhyme with "bomb"

7   Pronounced to rhyme with "float"

Many residents of the LOMB can be heard saying things like, "Wow, he's so smart. He went to an Ivy League school." or "He's such a good guy. He goes to church every Sunday." or "Did you see her house? She is doing so well." We all know that a good school, regular church attendance, and a beautiful home do not guarantee a financially or morally secure life.

If you are living in the professional LOMB, then you may work hard toward attaining a certain title only because it is coveted within your organization or circle. In the LOAT, you would refer to your value system, review your desired outcomes or sensations, and then determine if that title or career path is on your authentic path. In the same situation, you can have a different perspective depending upon whether you are living your truth or not.

Whenever unwanted feelings or sensations arise, you must immediately locate yourself in your truth to see where you are in relation to your own value system. If you realize you're not living according to your own value system, then it is time to revisit those values or make changes. You can work to identify these values at the end of the book. The goal is for them to be authentic to your personal truth.

People in the LOMB compare themselves to others because what matters in the LOMB is where you are in context to everyone else and the norms they've set. The use of the TPS is prohibited or rarely used in the LOMB. As you can imagine, it is very difficult to realize your own values when you own real estate in the LOMB. Not only is it difficult to stop and assess your values, they are also now irrelevant. Why would it matter that you value saving for your future if your values are developed from external sources that say what you have now is what matters most? If that's true, then you may take up the value of having possessions. How could you realize your professional purpose in life of being a web designer if you place great value in the LOMB on the field of medical sciences? Our knee-jerk reaction is to go where the "good" labels are.

The way to resist this is to dismiss the rules of play and the noise of the LOMB and apply your own values to achieve your desired sensations. Replacing society's expectations with your own values actually disqualifies you for life in the LOMB and makes you eligible for the LOAT. Remember, you can be in the LOMB in one area of your life and in the LOAT in another. The goal is to get to our authentic values in the LOAT in every area so that we do not try to take up residence in both places.

When you've lived in the LOAT for a significant period of time, you will be able to quickly locate yourself in the face of any situation, despite the reflex to be envious of others or harshly judge your own path. You can look at others' situations with a new lens—a lens that allows you to stay true to the facts and not speculate about how another person's life compares to yours. In addition, how other people live won't matter because the important thing is that you will know exactly how *you* want to live.

A comment often heard in the LOMB might be, "She has such a good job. I can't believe she didn't contribute to the fund-raiser." When you live in the LOAT, you know that we rarely know anyone's whole story, and therefore, you can reject the impulse to judge.

The LOAT is a place where truth is not judged but rather used to make decisions about our lives and futures that will benefit not only us but also everyone concerned. When you buy things you can't afford to keep up with the Joneses it rarely feels rewarding or fulfilling for long. It can actually be quite stressful. Chances are that you probably beat yourself up over the purchase because it wasn't really what you wanted to do. However, in that moment, your desire for the sensation of *acceptance* outweighed your value of saving.

When you make the transition into the LOAT, you start to make choices based on the life and values you've established for yourself rather than on those that external sources have placed upon you. You break free from the desire to be adorned with "good" societal labels. Residents in the LOAT stick with the facts, ask questions for understanding, and reserve opinions until more information can be obtained. They communicate their values and stand firmly by them even when circumstances aggressively challenge those values.

In many areas of our lives, we can choose to live in either the LOMB or the LOAT. We can live in the LOMB or the LOAT aesthetically, relationally, spiritually, emotionally, financially, professionally, and parentally. With so many opportunities to slip into the LOMB, keeping our TPSs (Truth-Positioning Systems) updated with our proper value coordinates is a necessary exercise to ensure fulfilling lives.

Now that you have a greater understanding of the roles the LOMB and the LOAT play in our life journeys, let's go forward to discuss our sensations and value systems.

* * *

Chapter 7 Reflections

- There are two places in which we can reside: LOMB (Land of Make-Believe) and LOAT (Land of Authenticity and Truth).

- The LOMB is the place where your life is based upon labels and is dependent upon perception.

- The LOAT is the place where decisions are based on your values and truth.

- In the LOMB, your life is held to external standards.

- In the LOAT, your life is held to your internal core values.

~ 8 ~

LIVING YOUR AESTHETIC TRUTH

The Sensation of Looking the Part

Thin. Well-rounded. Curvy. Shapely. Built. Buff. Muscular. Pudgy. Skinny. Fat. Pretty. Ugly. Average. Well-dressed. Homely. Corny. Cute. Handsome. Fine. Put together. Unattractive. Gorgeous.

We have so many terms to describe people's outward appearance. In addition to utilizing these terms, we take it a step further and label those terms good or bad. We go to great lengths to be included in one of the "good" categories. After all, who wants to be "bad"?

Our assignment of the label usually comes from society, and it's often assigned by various forms of media. In the United States, a narrow range of looks makes "the good list." Hollywood probably has the largest influence over decisions about what we should watch, what we should wear, how much we should weigh, and more. The images portrayed on the Internet, TV, and movies impregnate our minds with the "acceptable" looks and what those looks say about those who don them.

The most significant problem with the classification of looks or aesthetics is that it taps into our psyche, which has access to our feelings and affects our behavior. We end up treating people and being treated a certain way based solely upon aesthetics. We actually sum up the entire person in a glance. Statistics say this first impression happens within three to five seconds after seeing a person. The goal is to evolve to a truer existence by moving past our initial impressions and digging deeper before making a classification. We have to constantly recalibrate our minds to stay true to our values—particularly if we place any value on what people have to offer from their insides.

Except for holidays and special occasions, my mother did not often tell my sister, Tiffany, and me that we were pretty. She did, however, make a big deal about our good grades, problem-solving abilities, and kind gestures. She taught us to develop internal expectations for ourselves. What I learned about wanting nice clothing, having my hair done to perfection, and looking as nice as possible, I picked up outside of my home. Society taught me about living up to their external expectations. The fact that people are judged and treated according to something so unrelated to their character continues to cause quite a conflict for me.

Because of peer influences and pressures, I did become very aware and self-conscious about how I looked in my teen years, much to my mother's chagrin. My sister's and my desire for fashionable clothes was vetoed by my mother's desire to keep the mortgage paid. Buying designer clothes for her daughters was not on her list of priorities when she had our present education expenses to cover and our future education to save for. The convergence of my mother's influence and the expectations of my peers brought me to an interesting place. While I liked to dress nicely and have a "good" image, I did not want to be known simply for the way I dressed or how I looked. This never went away. I still value being well put together because I've learned that presentation is in my top five to seven core values, and I understand the power of perception. However, I'm not compelled to buy any particular handbag, shoe, or piece of clothing because it's new and/or the latest style. I buy what I like because I like it, no matter the label or cost.

Unfortunately, much of our society runs on a different value system. If you have the handbag everyone else is on a waiting list for, this possession increases your value. If you have the shoes that everyone else covets, this increases your value. If you wear name-brand clothing, this increases your value. If you are thin, this increases your value. If you are tall, this increases your value. Even as enlightened individuals who understand that these external things do not deserve such a high value, our immediate response is still to place a high value on them because the pressure to do so is deeply ingrained in our culture. However, the goal is to move past the initial inclination to place such a high value on the image and to dig deeper for meaning and understanding.

The problem with placing so much value on appearance is that it's temporary. We have all seen women both in the public's eye and in our own lives who are known and praised for their beauty. This emphasis often prompts them to put a high price on those looks. If a large value is attached to appearance, then when it begins to fade, the women's self-worth fades with it. We can see the evidence of this when the same women begin to have extensive plastic surgery and wear more youthful styles to hang on to their perceived value.

While studies have shown that men also suffer from image issues, the blow is softened by the fact that they are expected to become more handsome and more distinguished as they age, and more of their value is related to their ability to provide financially over how they look. These expectations carry their own weight, and men will sometimes succumb to altering their looks to ensure they are living up to social ideals.

We know that outer beauty is fleeting—it fades with time and circumstances—but we can still be driven by societal expectations. It is harder to remember that no matter how outwardly attractive you are or how well you dress, appearance pales in comparison to your inner spirit and unique talents.

I believe God's gifts—looks, talents, good fortune—should all be appreciated. If you receive welcomed attention because of your outward beauty, then relish it. Enjoy it. But don't depend on it. If you believe that your looks are critical to your true value, one day you will realize that they've depreciated, and what you will have left is your character—your talent, good habits, and well-established values. If you have developed these, they will serve you well as you mature and beyond.

Regardless of whether the mainstream values your looks or style, you must delve deeper into your own purpose and passion. Live from this deeper place and let the rest be a bonus. Even less-attractive people look better when their spirit is full of light and passion.

Getting past these narrow images of the "right" appearance will happen when we encourage the development of new media and hold existing media outlets accountable for portraying all types of images and not just ones that reflect their ideals of what is aesthetically acceptable.

I'm in no way encouraging you to dismiss the importance of dressing the part or looking your best. We have interviews to go to, parties to attend, jobs to keep, and eyes to catch. I'm only reminding you to keep your values at the forefront as you journey to your desired emotional sensations.

* * *

Sprinkling Pepper
In a world so focused on appearance, it can be difficult to find our own personal style and to align our values with the way we look. The external expectations can

91

be overwhelming; however, the benefits of staying true will leave you with less future regret.

* * *

Chapter 8 Reflections

- Base your aesthetic presentation on your personal values.

- Succumbing to trends leaves you vulnerable.

- Aesthetics can help you make a great first impression, but purpose, passion, and character will help you maintain a lasting impression.

~ 9 ~

LIVING YOUR
RELATIONAL TRUTH

The Sensation of Being Connected

No two people are perfect. However, this does not mean that relationships have to be dysfunctional by nature, just because two imperfect people are joining together.

Even with the divorce rate still hovering around 50 percent and the number of outrageous stories reported in the media regarding relationship matters (both platonic and romantic), I'm confident we can find a better way. I believe providing formal teaching on value identification and human relations in our formative years would assist us in addressing this problem. Currently, it's left up to trial and error.

We have many different kinds of relationships: parent and child, friend and friend, employer and employee, partner and partner, girlfriend and boyfriend, husband and wife, just to name a few. No matter how intimate the relationship, it should never indicate to either party a sense of ownership. Effective relationships are mutually beneficial and based on some critical shared values.

Of course, we all live in the real world, and we can understand that people will create functional relationships that are in no way based on shared values but rather on the filling of a void. These are, in most cases, short-term relationships or long arduous ones. Even in these relationships, communication is key. If someone is providing you with the attention you desire but not the shared values, you have to be honest about the future of the connection. This is important because when one party believes the relationship is moving toward a long-term status while the other believes it is merely a short-term situation, someone is going to get hurt. We've all seen movies or TV shows depict a break-up with the person being dumped saying, "I thought we were in this together" or "I thought we were working on something more." This is what happens when two people have two different sets of expectations and do not communicate.

After getting my first job as a health care benefits analyst, I remember saying, "I love my job!" And I told everyone about it. I was smitten. The job was new, the people were nice, the work was challenging, the money was beyond my expectations, and the job created a form of independence for me that I craved. Over time, however, my feelings for the job began to change. I no longer felt that I loved my job, and I actually began to loathe going to work every day. I couldn't explain why at the time, but I have come to understand that this happened gradually as my values weren't being met in that job. They are the same values I have today of autonomy, consideration, open-mindedness, creativity, variety, presentation, and problem solving.

In one of my positions, a very clear vision had been set by the head of human resources and had to be realized, so achieving autonomy was out. The set hours for work were 9:00 a.m. to 5:00 p.m., so variety was out. The products we were offering were standardized, so creativity was out in this regard. Every report was created from a template, so variety was out. I was responsible for setting plans to assist clients in reducing healthcare costs, so problem solving was in. Only one of my values was included in my daily work, and it just wasn't a big enough part of my job to keep me satisfied.

These values also ring true for me in relationships. I once had a long-term relationship with a gentleman I was very infatuated with and liked a lot. He was handsome, which was nice, but not necessarily required for my attraction to him. He had a great sense of humor and we had lots of laughs, which was also nice. He checked on me to make sure I was OK when I was away from him, and he didn't blindly make decisions that affected me without my input, both of which showed consideration. He wanted to always know what I was doing and who I was with, which meant I had a decreased sense of autonomy. We didn't share many of the same interests. He was content to live and work at the same place without planning for anything different, so that challenged my value of creativity. And, when I told him about a few shenanigans from my past, he passed judgment, which meant I was not comfortable sharing anything more from my life. Open-mindedness was out.

So, you can see that things started off great. However, over time the benefits were outweighed by the value compromises. I began to feel trapped. I had to get out.

The process to decide to end a relationship isn't easy. It requires attention, focus, and honesty. You have to look inside yourself and inside your relationship, whether it is romantic or platonic. Values must be considered to understand if they are aligned or complementary enough to be in a romantic or platonic relationship. Given that romantic relationships usually require spending more time together than platonic ones, it is more critical that the values come together. The volume can be turned down on the amount of time you spend with platonic friends, allowing the possibility of keeping certain friends even with only a few aligned values.

This process also applies to platonic friendships. Michelle Ventor summed it up nicely when she wrote a poem that was circulating the internet in the early 2000's. She wrote that people are in your life for a reason, a season, or a lifetime. Values are the determining factor for the health and/or longevity of relationships. As I quoted before, "Do two walk together unless they have agreed to do so?"[8] When shared values are the guiding light on the path, two people can walk together. When one person on the journey begins to walk the path of the other, then resentment can creep in over time. When resentment creeps in, respect begins to diminish, and this leads to lashing out.

Here are my final points on this: Be careful what you sign up for in relationships, platonic or romantic. Identify your

---

8   Amos 3:3

values. Don't apologize for them. Take time to see through the sparkly sensations to the person that you are with.

* * *

Think about some of the best times you've had. Maybe it's hanging out with your mother or going to baseball games with your grandfather, taking walks with your significant other, vacationing with friends, or some other scenario. Most of our favorite times are those shared with someone else. Of course, we can have amazingly insightful times alone—times of self-reflection and soul work, which I encourage; however, we are born to be in relationship to other people, to be connected to one another in a variety of ways: mother to child, friend to friend, peer to peer, manager to subordinate, husband to wife, and even stranger to stranger. We need to be in relationships with other people, and we actually need human touch to thrive. A great deal of research confirms the correlation between human touch and health and happiness. They're all related.

One of the ways our human relationships are suffering in this age of social media is our dependence on technology to deliver our messages. Rather than interact in person, or even by telephone, we are communicating our personal and important information via text and email—breakups, death notifications, firings, and other sensitive topics. While we could make an argument for the benefit of being able to impart this information quickly and only once, what we are losing is the opportunity to let our friends help us through our hurts with kindly spoken words and gentle touches.

When we are young, we learn how to be in relationships through our interactions with people, our experiences in life, advice from our elders, and what we are able to glean for ourselves along the way. Since the majority of our understanding about how to manage relationships comes from trial and error, it behooves us to communicate with the people we are in relationships with so we have an idea about how we're doing. Many of us know adults who have never mastered the art of communication in relationships. Either they don't communicate well with others, or others don't communicate well with them. Some of this comes from misaligned values. It is difficult for us to receive feedback that says we're less than extraordinary, but learning from this kind of feedback is the only way we can develop and grow.

As we go through life, we continue to develop relationships. Some we value. Others we may not. Either way, not all relationships are created equal. For example, the relationship we may have with a significant other is not likely to be the same as the relationship we have with our mail carrier. We can have a variety of friends and acquaintances, and we can value those relationships in different ways.

We usually determine the value of each relationship by the value alignment—level of communication, exchange, and intimacy—between ourselves and the other person. For instance, our connection to a parent may be deeper, and often more valuable, than that of a coworker because we have shared more intimate experiences with our parent than with our co-worker. "That exchange creates value in an emotional bank account," Stephen Covey, author of *The Seven Habits of Highly Effective People* and other self-help books, says. Much like a regular bank account, where people deposit and withdraw money, we also have an emotional bank account into which we make deposits and withdrawals. The more deposits we make through caring, sharing, and being there for one another, the higher our value and the more connected we become.

Stephen Covey also makes the point that one of the best ways to continue to build solid and valuable relationships is to "seek first to understand, then to be understood." When we approach our relationships in this manner, we can make more informed decisions about how to move forward with the exchange or even if we should move forward at all. Through honesty, understanding, and communication, we can create meaningful exchanges. If we try to move forward in a relationship without understanding what our partner expects, we are setting ourselves up for failure. It can be compared to walking blindfolded through an unfamiliar home and trying to find the kitchen. We would bump into doors, fixtures, and furniture because we would have no sense of how to get to our destination. Failure is almost guaranteed. Relationships should be mutually beneficial, and not all relationships are treated equally. The point is to ensure that over time the exchanges don't deplete either party's emotional bank account for any significant period of time.

Living your most authentic life in relationships requires you to go through a discovery process. Start by identifying your values. This will help you to understand your desired truth, sensations, and emotions. Once you have achieved this, you can locate your true self and start living your truth based on your values.

* * *

Sprinkling Pepper

Acceptance of one's truth is a critical component to building trust and longevity in human relationships, and so is acceptance of others' truths. Deciding to label or judge someone because of differing value systems is a quick way to short-circuit a potentially rewarding relationship. People know when others aren't interested in understanding their truths, and they withdraw from those who are quick to judge them. We find this in everything from marriages to business negotiations. Seek first to understand, then to be understood.

* * *

Familial Relationships: Is Blood Thicker than Water?

You would probably think family relationships are the easiest place to be authentic since your family members are the people who believe they know you best. However, the fact that they've known you so long is one of the main reasons why communicating your truth to them can be more difficult. They "knew you when," so they assume they already understand your core values and truth. They remember when you used to bully people, lived a particular lifestyle, dated a certain type of person, dressed a certain way, and more. They were there. They remember, and they will remind you.

It doesn't matter when you come to understand your truth and your values; your family will take a little longer to come around to believing you and accepting them. They may never come around. In this case, your family history could be the very thing that keeps these relationships out of the realm of truth and unable to move forward. People in general may get on your nerves and irritate you for any number of reasons, and family is no exception. Just because you have the same blood running through your veins doesn't mean you have the same value system. They say that we can choose our friends, but we can't choose our family. However, we can choose new family members to supplement our sense of family. I have many people in my "family" who are not biologically related to me.

Should the opportunity arise, try to communicate your changing values and your truth to your family, but remember to handle them with care. These relationships are actually more fragile than we expect, particularly for the reason I mentioned above: They believe they know you better than you know yourself.

* * *

Friendships: The Salt of the Earth

Precious, precious friendships. In addition to God, my friendships represent a foundational necessity in my life. Due to my history of not fully attaching, I haven't always been the best at nurturing friendships; however, at this point in my life, I am fully aware of what they offer: growth, development, fulfillment, connection, and more. And I want all of it. I love my friends. I mean, really! They provide analysis, care, challenges, humor, guidance, an ear when needed, support and more. They keep me honest when I accidentally slip into the LOMB because they know how hard I've worked to get out. They listen to my slip-ups and give me honest and thoughtful feedback. They are open, and they care about the issues of this world. I mean, I just can't say enough. My friends aren't perfect, but they rock! Let me add here that not all of the people I thought of as friends made it to my new home in the LOAT. On this journey to authentic living, you'll need to prepare for those who are not going to be able to walk with you because their values don't align or because they are unaware of their residence in the LOMB.

Now, with that being said, maintaining great friendships can take work. And by work, I mean communication. Building or maintaining great friendships is sometimes easy and sometimes hard. Time spent and information exchanged are like deposits to the emotional bank account and are factors that help determine the depth of the relationship. Not every friend is on a journey to truth, and we can respect that because we weren't always on this journey either. And if we have friends who are searching out their truth, that doesn't mean we will be able to travel together at this point.

This dynamic can cause many hurt feelings throughout Friendship Land, especially for those who feel the need to be great friends with everyone they meet. This need may represent an area of truth that needs to be addressed. If you recognize this need in yourself, revisit your sensations and find out what's behind your desire for so many close friends. You may simply be that outgoing and friendly, or you may be trying to live up to a label from the LOMB. Take the time to determine your desired sensations and identify your values. Seek first to understand and then to be understood. In the face of any circumstances, stay true to your values.

Imagine you're in a conversation with a group of people and someone begins to speak poorly of someone you know. Your value of consideration should keep you from joining in and may even cause you to defend the person being maligned. Now, this could cause an uncomfortable place for the person who started the conversation, you, and anyone else who may be near enough to hear. If you can communicate clearly and from a place of truth to your value system—with respect for both the person being discussed and the person doing the discussing—the ripple in the friendship can be short-lived. You can stick to your values while still being respectful. Over time, you will have communicated your values well enough through word and deed that hopefully your true friends will not include you in these kinds of conversations. You may have friends who, in an attempt to respect your values, may opt to exclude you from certain invitations. While you may have hurt feelings initially, it actually shows that they are respecting your values. You *want* to be excluded from situations that are misaligned with your values.

Some people don't have the same need to always be included. However, you can still challenge yourself to identify your values in the same way and to stand firm in the face of social pressure. One common value challenge often shows up when friends or acquaintances start speaking of women, either generally or specifically. A friend may urge you to degrade or speak ill of a woman because of her behavior or her appearance. However, because you value honesty and respect, you can make the choice to stand firm in those values and not join in. The value compromise may also rear its ugly head when you are making decisions about work or feeling the need for material things. If you stand firm and stay true to your values, you will find that your true friends will support you.

You will have friends who can function in any situation. Whether you take them to a seedy neighborhood or the penthouse suite, they will engage with everyone and anyone. Others will be comfortable in only one or just a few settings. You may have friends who travel in the same style you do and others who do not. You may have friends who are extremely judgmental and label everything in their path, which may keep you from telling them as much as you want. At the end of the day, if you've named someone a friend, that person has earned it in some way and therefore has some credit in your emotional bank account.

It is important for you to have a great understanding of your own personal values so you can be clear about your hot buttons. When you find you have become irritated or upset, examine the true cause. It's often because something has collided with your value system. When you can recognize the cause, you can make better decisions about how to deal with it. One option is to tell the person who hit your value hot button how it made you feel and that you would like that area to be handled with a bit more care in the future. Keep in mind that the person most likely doesn't share that same value and therefore may not fully understand the magnitude of the value they just confronted for you.

You can also share your values with the person. Many of your friends will want to understand and will stay away from actions that cause conflict. At a minimum, your friend will have greater understanding of the source of your irritation. Of course, the approach you use to handle the situation is yours. You may choose to simply disengage, although that is not what I recommend.

* * *

Sprinkling Pepper
Remember that you want your friends to respect your values, even if they don't share them.

* * *

And now I would like to address the subject of taking offense in relationships. Offense has the potential to create large wedges in relationships. It often takes place when we feel slighted or as if someone is attacking us in some way. For instance, if one friend invites another friend to a gathering and doesn't invite you, your first reaction may be to take offense. However, you should take some time to consider before acting on that feeling. Offense is a self-centered emotion. It assumes that we are at the center of the situation rather than recognizing that others are simply doing what's best for them or saying how they really feel. What we have to take stock of is our level of comfort with our decisions, our actions, our being, and ourselves.

Take a moment to recognize that no matter how close the friendship, none of us is made for every situation. I know it's hard to believe, but despite how amazing you are, there will be times when your presence is neither requested nor required. For example, I fully understand that everyone doesn't always need or want my positive outlook or to hear how the right approach can turn a bad situation around. Sometimes people just want to dwell in their circumstances and have their friends commiserate. Sometimes people just want the company of each other without me. No offense need be taken. I'm comfortable enough with myself not to take it personally. If I believe that I've done something to cause the situation, then I simply address it.

You may feel offense when someone says something generalized that you feel is a personal attack. For instance, your friend may say, "It's so stupid how much money people spend on shoes," without any regard for the fact that you are a person who has been known to spend a lot of money on shoes. You may feel offended. In this case, it seems that offense would come if only you are personally uncomfortable with how much you spend on shoes. Otherwise, it would just be someone's opinion, which we all have a right to. When we are comfortable with who we are, our values, and how we move about the world, there is less room for offense. Comfort and offense cannot coexist. When the spirit of offense creeps in, we must identify the source and gain understanding why the action evoked the feeling.

On the other side of offense, we have intentions, which are important as we seek understanding. Just as we have the opportunity to be offended by misinterpreting someone else's intentions, we must also examine our own intentions when communicating. Sometimes our own discomfort with ourselves can cause us to say and/or do things that we know are hurtful. Perhaps we know someone who is working to gain comfort and confidence in a certain area of expertise. If that person has said or done something to cause us to have a value confrontation, we may develop intentions to drag that person down rather than build our friend up. In these situations, we might be tempted to say something that we know will make our friend feel uncomfortable. This is just one example of a situation in which we need to calm down and examine our own motivations and values before we act out.

In the event that you are curious about someone else's intentions, you can start the conversation by asking about it. It is important to address conflict before it turns into resentment. While the conversation may not be easy, it is key to maintaining your good friendships.

For instance, if someone tells us, respectfully, that something we said was rude, but we know we didn't intend to be rude, we can simply address it, apologize, and consider it later. The point is to understand if it was a value confrontation or a one-off situation. However, if several people regularly tell us that we are rude, it may be time to consider the way we choose our words and try to find some truth and growth in the exploration.

Suppose someone refers to you as snobby. Before becoming offended, you need to understand the value filter from which the other person is processing your decisions or actions. The only way to do this is to communicate. Your questions might be, "What about me or my actions would lead you to believe that I'm snobby?" Listen intently to the answer for behaviors. This will be your indicator of the filter used to categorize your behaviors as snobby. Your next move is to say

"Thank you for making the emotional investment of giving me your thoughts." Finally, assuming you care enough about the relationship to do so, acknowledge your friend's value approach and offer some understanding into your own value approach. You might say, "I completely appreciate you sharing that with me. I now have a better understanding your value filter. Would you mind if I share my experience with you?"

This may sound corny, but when it comes to relationship building, understanding each other's core value approach will eliminate many offenses along the way. It creates a space for connecting and meeting the other person at the values and not at the offense.

My connection to this is very personal. I had a friend who labeled me as snobby. I was not offended as much as I wondered what I'd done to warrant the label, particularly because of how much I value open-mindedness. So, I asked her about the label. At the time, we were driving around in my car. My friend wanted to turn the music up—beyond a level I was comfortable with—because it was one of her favorite songs. I immediately turned it down and said, "That's too loud."

She laughed condescendingly and said, "You're so snobby."

Given that we were in the moment, I felt it necessary to gain understanding, so I asked, "Why, because I don't want to play the music loud for everyone to hear?"

She said, "Yes."

I said, "Well, consideration is a core value of mine and it feels completely inconsiderate, by my definition, to impose my music, conversation, etc. on other people."

We ended up laughing about it and gained a stronger friendship because we took the time to talk it over.

I have had other experiences when the conversation didn't go so smoothly, and the other person's values were in such conflict with mine that my point was lost. These are the moments that we can release offense and capture understanding. I understood that that person and I could not walk together.

Relationships require communication. Communication requires understanding. Understanding requires self-reflection. Self-reflection requires truth.

* * *

Business Relationships: The Ultimate Truth Test

Navigating your value system and your truth while working to create opportunities for your livelihood can get very hairy. Given our society's value placement on status and on succeeding in business, slipping into the position of value compromise becomes very easy. In the business environment, expectations and labels run rampant. You're expected to perform, be quick, socialize, strategize, solve problems, create, develop, run meetings, manage, and more. A few promotions and a little praise from the right people can quickly move our own values into second place and the company's values into first. This is a great example of chasing the labels.

Before you start any job, it is wise to have a good grasp on your values, your desired truth, and the authentic values of the organization. That last one will take some research on your part. Going on the organization's website is a good first step, but it is insufficient. With a little investigation, you can usually find a difference in the company's listed values and the values they actually practice within the organization. A good second step would be to talk with people who already work there and find out what they think. Having this understanding will be your "truth star," through the complicated world of business where relationships and perceptions can be paramount to your success. Understanding your own values will allow you to stand firm on them when various situations arise that challenge your truth. While the journey to living out your values in professional relationships may be rocky at the start, the road will eventually smooth out.

A great way to introduce your values is by establishing authentic relationships with various people in your organization. Be honest with your co-workers, and ignore the labels that appear on the surface. This builds trust, understanding, and respect. In business relationships, it can be easier for two people with very different value platforms find a way to walk together. The emotions don't run as high here because the common goal is the business objective.

On one occasion when I had to stand up for my values at work, I did so by explaining my position and why it meant so much to me. My colleague stood firm on his position and in his value—until he heard me. While everything we valued in this situation still wasn't the same, we did agree that the one thing we shared was the desire for the team's success. After starting the conversation again from this place of truth and commonality, we were able to move forward quite easily. Taking the initiative to start these conversations, keeping your goals in view, and making sure your pride does not get in your way will catapult you into a successful, respected, and authentic position.

On another occasion, I had the facilitator of a sales training course suggest a certain method I should use to handle cold calls. From my perspective, the call technique he suggested appeared to mislead the person on the other end of the phone. While the facilitator was encouraging me to compromise my value of consideration so I could make more connections and more money, I was more comfortable with my own system. By remaining true to my definition of my value, I achieved the sensation of *assuredness*.

We've all heard the saying "It's not about what you know, but who you know." I would like to submit that it's not just about who you know but who knows you and how that person knows you. When you introduce your value system in your business relationships early, it allows you to build a mutual respect with your bosses, co-workers, and employees, even if you have conflicting value systems. Many people end up hating their jobs because of the value compromises they've had to make in order to keep their positions. Their lack of fulfillment is not typically described as a value disparity; it is more usually displayed with a constant stream of complaints about management, co-workers, and company policies. When we consult our value systems, we can avoid complaining and make positive changes in our lives and our relationships.

Because of the pressures and expectations to perform and to be accepted in the business world, many of us feel as if we have to join individuals of influence to get ahead, even if it means a compromise in our value systems. Just as in our other relationships, we have to find a way to be true to our own values without being disrespectful of the others in our business community.

* * *

Sprinkling Pepper

We all encounter many forks in the road in this journey called life. Navigating in a business environment will certainly present circumstances that demand that we take a stand for our truth. Being converted to another

person's value system each time will surely leave us with the sensation of *disappointment*.

* * *

Sometimes, in our quest to rise up the ranks or land a new client, we let our agenda supersede our value system. As a rising star in an organization or a new entrepreneur who would like to establish relevant relationships to support growth, the goal of establishing relationships with the "right" people may trigger some LOMB behavior. We might come to believe that we need to be connected to a particular person in order to move ahead, despite a significant conflict between our values and those of the other person. We might disregard the clear misalignment of our values and proceed in an inauthentic way to establish a relationship anyway. We might even begin to take on certain traits of that person so we can be seen in a different light.

Ultimately, these behaviors will lead to an internal conflict because we can only hold back our truth temporarily. Eventually, our real selves will be seen and heard.

I've worked in corporate, entertainment, entrepreneurial, and nonprofit environments, and one thing holds true in all of them: politics and egos are ever present. You have to perform a balancing act in those environments if you are to remain connected with your truth. Sometimes this means that you don't reach the finish line as fast as you think you should have or that you aren't part of the "in crowd." Sometimes it means that you have to search a little longer for the right work environment and/or clients. These are short-term sacrifices for your long-term fulfillment.

We often feel that quicker is better, but if we know how to negotiate a certain type of contract today rather than to-morrow or next week, what does that mean? The result may be that we make more money a few days sooner than we would have made it anyway. Anyone on the outside looking in might be impressed with how fast we got where we want-ed to be, but how much value does someone else's opinion actually have?

Take *your* road. Longer could mean stronger. Someone who endures and makes it certainly has proven a certain lev-el of fortitude and tenacity, and that has value, too. Focus on the path that will lead to your desired sensations. When you find an area you happen to be quick in, enjoy it. Remember that some skills will come easily, while others will require greater effort to get the result you want.

Be yourself and hold tightly to what you believe. If integrity is one of your values, then don't try to up-sell your client out of their price range, even if a higher-up within your organization suggests it. If excellence is one of your values, then don't take a shortcut when you think no one will notice, even if it will make you more money.

Truth has a way of finding you, and what you sow is what you will reap.

* * *

On Embarking on Romantic Relationships: The Beginning

Many of the foundational elements that come into play in our romantic relationships came from what we saw growing up and from our own past experiences. We tend to react out of love or fear. If we feel we deserve love and respect, then we expect and even demand it from our partners; if we feel unworthy of being treated with love and respect, then we may allow people to mistreat us. We may be disrespectful to our significant others because we witnessed this form of behavior while growing up and believe it to be the right way to talk to the people we love.

When our love isn't returned, many of us may panic or feel unworthy as we feel the sensation of *rejection*. That reaction may stem from being abandoned by a parent or another significant person earlier in our lives. To avoid this sensation, we may manipulate our significant others with false flattery, guilt, jealousy, or some other means. Perhaps we witnessed that behavior growing up or perhaps we learned it along the way, but it is important to remember that manipulation is not a path to truth. We need to utilize effective communication skills and knowledge to create a foundation from which to build. We have to make an effort to understand the other person's needs prior to trying to satisfy our own. This will yield far greater relational returns.

If you discover through communication that your values are misaligned, don't ignore this. Maya Angelou said, "When someone shows you who they are, believe them the first time." Explaining away your significant person's authentic truth or simply pretending not to see it doesn't change anything. It is through the aligning of values that we locate the relationship that will give us understanding on how to proceed.

Before deciding whether to enter into a romantic relationship, it helps to give the relationship time to breathe and air out your respective values before you enter in for the long haul. If you regard attention, dependability, quality time, service to others, and spirituality as your core values, your potential mate needs to know that. And you need to know your partner's values as well.

In addition to identifying your values, you both need to understand each other's personal definitions of what those values mean. Dependability to you may mean doing what you say you will do when you say you will do it. To your significant other, it may mean eventually doing what you say you will do—when you get to it. In both scenarios, the task will get done, but the misalignment in the definition will certainly cause stress in the relationship. Both of you may think the definition is obvious, but until it is stated plainly, neither of you will really understand what the other one means. You may have experienced that simple conversation that suddenly escalated to a heated debate. When two people have different definitions of the same value, communication is strained. A casual comment can turn into an argument, spurred on by the sensation of *frustration*.

Gaining an understanding of the truth each person desires in the relationship is important for both parties. You have to know if it is acceptance, admiration, respect, or some other sensation you seek. You also have to locate the truth in the relationship you need and compare that to your current position in the relationship you are in. Ask yourself if this relationship is meeting your values. Analyze what you and your significant other have shared, and ask yourself, *Will we both be able to achieve our truths in this relationship?*

This is where the choice between living in the LOMB or the LOAT comes to the forefront. You have to be careful that you don't let your need for the sensation of love, admiration, or any other sensation elevate your potential mate above your values. While in the beginning you may be starry-eyed about the sensations this person evokes for you, these things quickly fade when you are continually disappointed by your partner who is simply displaying his or her own values that may not match your own. Sparkly things like love, admiration, and other shiny sensations begin to fade when our values are being compromised.

It is critical that we take a look at all our core values to see where our values and those of our significant other align. If we value spirituality as a core value and our potential mate doesn't, we have to decide if we can accept that or if the misalignment of that value is a deal-breaker. We're not reaching for perfection, but we do have to know which inconsistencies we can live with.

This is all important soul work that needs to be done. Think for a moment about what happens when a new person comes into your life. The person makes you laugh and feel happy, possibly breaking up the monotony of your life. This person is sexually and emotionally attractive to you and finds you attractive as well. The excitement of the new relationship is inspiring big dreams for both of you, which makes the future feel very exciting. And, of course, the person pays a great deal of attention to you, which makes you feel important. So, we have the person filling the following voids: happiness, attraction, excitement, and attention.

What happens when the process of living changes everything? Perhaps your happy new person becomes depressed and no longer makes you laugh, or gains weight and becomes less attractive to you, or settles down and has dreams more in line with routine living, or gets caught in the daily grind, which causes less attention to come your way. How will it affect your feelings toward the person when one or all of the void fillers are no longer present?

An emotional slaughter occurs when you attach your feelings to the function a person serves in your life instead of to the person and the value alignment that the two of you share. Function and value are *not* the same. When the person you're functionally attached to no longer serves in that capacity, the relationship suddenly becomes unfulfilling. When you value the actual person and the values you share, then the uncertain variables in life do not cause you to lose your connection.

When a relationship ends, many people will ask, "What happened to the love?" The answer usually lies in the fact that the relationship was based on function, not on an authentic connection rooted in shared values. Love is not the question.

For the connection to remain, values must be aligned. If someone you truly love and value as a human being loses a job, stops buying you flowers, gets busy, has a bout with depression, or is otherwise unable to serve a particular function, the connection remains. The loss or reduction of the function the person serves in your life will cause some stress, but the stress is more about locating the person in relation to the change. In a values-based relationship, you check in to see if the person no longer wants to serve that function or is simply unable to do so because of the circumstances. As partners, we must assist. Notice that this is often the opposite of what often happens when we lose the connection, when the function is no longer being served.

When I was in my twenties, I struggled with the idea of dating several people at a time. I was more of a one-guy-at-a-time kind of girl. I couldn't comprehend accepting multiple offers. Something about it felt inappropriate. I now believe that it was those societal expectations that were placed upon me that prevailed. Now that I am a divorced woman in my 40s, I understand. I no longer feel the need to choose one and only one from the beginning. I believe that you can build friendships with multiple people until you find the person you want to commit to romantically or that you can recognize "the one" quickly and decide to commit early. My point is that there is no right or wrong answer. It's a personal journey.

I had the pleasure of meeting three very different men after my divorce. Each of these men brought something special to my life, but none of them ultimately aligned with my values for a long-term, stable relationship.

It is perfectly okay to enjoy the function a person serves in your life while continuing to understand that their values simply don't line up with yours enough to create a true connection. It works best, when everyone understands that. The start-up infatuation is wonderful, but it is not a solid base upon which to build a long-lasting relationship.

When you look deeper into the values that you share with your potential mate, you may discover that the presence of some of your core values outweigh the need for all of them. This would suggest that you've really narrowed down what your true top core values are. When it comes to relationships, this is where understanding your top three to five values is critical. Keep in mind that over time the truth may change for one or both of you. When and if it does, communication is the only way to maintain and continue to build your relationship. However, when you find that your values are not aligned, that may be a more difficult obstacle to overcome. Identify and communicate your respective values early.

* * *

Continuing Romantic Relationships: When You're Already There

After being in a romantic relationship for some time, new truths may arise. This realization of truth can usually be recognized in the form of a rising level of dissatisfaction or resentment in your relationship. As soon as you can clearly communicate these changes with your partner, you should initiate a discussion. If the foundation of your relationship includes honest communication, you can communicate this new development with your partner. If the two of you have not already developed effective communication skills, now is a great time to start. When you're in an unfulfilling relationship, the first step is to revisit your values and truths. The next step is to discuss them with your partner.

Before even trying to communicate what the "issues" are, start by talking about what you both value. This can help illustrate your common ground as a couple before introducing the areas where your values part ways. Although you may believe you know everything about your mate, you may learn things about your significant other that you did not know, and things may be revealed to both of you that are totally new during this exchange. If you are both open and can embrace some of each other's new truths, this could be an incredible time for growth; it is also kind of sexy! Nothing stimulates a relationship like the joy of new discoveries.

Be careful not to let old hurts that were inflicted by your past cloud your ability or availability to listen. If you learn that your mate values knowledge and you don't share that in your top five to seven values, don't disregard it. Gain further understanding from your mate on how that value might be lived out. Does it mean your mate wants to go to school full-time, wants to find more time to read, envisions the two of you taking classes together, or something else? Decide if you can support your mate's value of knowledge in the way it is envisioned. This may be a very simple example, but these are the kinds of things that can drive wedges in relationships. Truth changes things. You'll have to determine how.

If your spouse suddenly wants to pursue a new venture, job, or hobby that you don't agree with, your initial reaction should not be a discouraging explanation of all of the reasons why it is a bad idea. Instead, you should take a moment to consider the Stephen Covey philosophy I mentioned before: "Seek first to understand and then to be understood." Listen to the reasons your spouse wants to do it, with a mind that is open to a different point of view. At first, the new direction might seem irresponsible, but maybe your spouse is trying to elevate his or her value of provision, flexibility, or freedom. If you have an understanding of your spouse's value system, you can support your partner in a way that works for your whole family without labeling the change as irresponsible. Keep in mind, this applies only if the value is in line with or complementary to your value system, too. If you have a value in direct conflict, you will need to keep the discussion going until you can find a working solution together.

Another example: If your spouse has spending habits that stress you out, you can take a moment to understand why your partner is spending so much instead of just complaining about it. If you remain in the philosophy of seeking first to understand, you may learn that your partner didn't know money was tight, that the car had been having trouble, that the kids had a sudden growth spurt and needed new clothes in the middle of the year, or that the home office needed a new organizational system. If you make an effort to understand your partner's values and then share yours as soon as the spending gets out of control, then you increase the likelihood of gaining greater understanding and compromise.

When we have negative reactions to the way our significant other expresses a value we don't share, we can expect a negative reaction in return. In true human nature fashion, this begins a loop of unproductive communication and lack of understanding. It may also shut down the communication process altogether. We all tend to have negative reactions when our core values are confronted in a negative way.

* * *

Sprinkling Pepper

When we don't agree with someone's choices or values, jumping right in to chastise or label the person only creates a defensive state. Once this state has been achieved, the communication process is aborted, and it becomes very difficult to return to an effective problem-solving state. We can all remember a time when we were judged and how that treatment made us feel. We have to listen for understanding. Live true!

* * *

Romantic relationships are tricky when begun with evasiveness and simple when begun with truth. We have all been told, "If you really love someone, then you can make it through anything," but we know that this just isn't true. Love can conquer many things; however, it cannot guarantee that your relationship will make it through everything. I've seen people who really, really love each other go their separate ways in love. Love can make you listen with an understanding ear. Love can allow you to let the relationship end when it is over. Love can keep you from hurting someone's feelings or casually disposing of them when your truth has changed. Love cannot make you share the same values. Love cannot stop an addiction. Love cannot bring back romantic love that has turned platonic.

It takes two people to participate in a fulfilling romantic relationship. The value exchange has to happen, the earlier the better. When both parties are honest, the value exchange helps one person know what's really important to the other. Only once you have a chance to truly understand your partner's values can you have clarity on whether or not to move forward. Even when we try to convince ourselves to believe we can deal with a misalignment of values, when we have too many misalignments, a break-up or an unfulfilling relationship is the most likely result.

I was married for nine years and am now divorced. I speak with a great many people in various types of relationships. I am convinced that foundational work, value alignment, and a high level of healthy communication will determine the health of any relationship, whether it is romantic or platonic. A high level of communication includes not just sharing wants, needs, and pet peeves, but also defining terms for each person. Both partners may value friendship, for instance, but the definition of friendship varies from person to person. Understanding how each value is defined by each person will help enable clearer, more effective communication.

These conversations also provide an opportunity to learn about each other's emotional baggage. When you get involved with someone who has no idea about your values, buttons will unknowingly be pushed. If you don't do the foundational work of understanding, then these accidental button-pushes can turn into major issues.

Living your romantic relational truth requires just that—truth! You first have to tell yourself the truth and then communicate it to the other person.

It would be hard for me to leave this section of the chapter without addressing the situation of living in the middle of a lie. I'm talking about holding on for dear life to a situation that is killing your soul. While each situation is different, I do know what it feels like to be in a place that barely resembles the vision you had for yourself, your relationship, or your values. Since you are the only one who knows your circumstances, the only advice I can offer is this: Identify your values, determine your truth, communicate your needs, assess your situation, and make a decision. Sometimes the answer is to leave the relationship; sometimes the answer is to examine your own behavior and expectations to see if the problem lies within. The whole point of knowing your values is so that you can be clear when the alignment just isn't there and thus knowing when it is time to move on.

Take some time to sit with yourself and invest in some much-needed self-reflection. During that time, think about your values, truth, and baggage. Don't dwell on the baggage; just identify it. Be honest about any functions your significant other is serving and about what would be left if those functional things no longer remained. The point of identifying your baggage is to gain understanding of your emotional hot buttons. These are the circumstances that cause your baggage (emotional wounds) to be front and center. Here is where internal scars versus value misalignment may account for the breakdown of a relationship. The point of this is to know when it is *your* "stuff" that is getting in the way and not that of your significant other.

* * *

Sprinkling Pepper

Remember that we are a people in transition looking for ways to live honestly and more authentically. Don't fight the growth. While our family might think we've lost our marbles, we're actually collecting a brand-new and complete set.

* * *

Chapter 9 Reflections

- The best relationships are some form of partnership with no elements of ownership.

- Align your values with those you are in relationships with to realize the true connection.

- Seek to understand the values of others, instead of judging them for having them.

- Resentment will come when core values are compromised.

- Move forward with relationships when values are aligned or complementary.

- Relationships require communication. Communication requires understanding. Understanding requires self-reflection. Self-reflection requires truth

~ 10 ~

LIVING YOUR SPIRITUAL TRUTH

The Sensation of Centeredness

While I believe that I've embarked on an authentic journey to my spiritual center, I cannot provide an ABCs of Spiritual Enlightenment here; the journey is too personal to apply a one-size-fits-all philosophy. However, I will share my journey to the amazingly connected and centered spiritual life I now live, in hopes that you will be encouraged to continue searching until you find the way that works for you.

I grew up in a conservative African Methodist Episcopal church in Philadelphia called New Bethel AME in Germantown. While many of the members were very serious and reserved, this atmosphere didn't keep my mother, my younger sister, and I from having a good laugh in church on a regular basis. We were filled with joy and found giggles everywhere we looked.

My sister and I participated in nearly every aspect of church because our mother signed us up for everything—Christmas and Easter plays, announcements, Sunday school, church retreats, the choir, bake sales, usher board, visiting other churches to represent ours, and anything else the church could think of for youth involvement. The high level of participation taught us about God, Jesus, the Bible, and the caring and nurturing environment of which we were a part. We were members of a church family, and I loved them.

While I couldn't fully appreciate it then, I could never deny the role this institution played in the development of my spiritual values. I learned about love, caring for others, sacrifice, discipline, and more. I also learned about the importance of encouraging people when they are having a rough go in life, about not judging others and their circumstances, and about giving to others in need. The foundation for the spiritual muscles I currently possess was established at this AME church.

My sister and I still enjoy reminiscing about the people, songs, and situations that we enjoyed in our childhood church. These shared experiences are part of what ties us together.

I attended that church until I left for Hampton University, and I thought I was ready to spread my spiritual wings away from home. I attended church on campus, but only if I hadn't stayed out too late the night before. I continued my prayer life, but only when I was worried about a test or wanted a certain young man on campus to notice me. These kinds of things certainly kept my practice of prayer alive, but my spiritual life was considerably less active than before I'd arrived at Hampton.

After I graduated from college, I continued to have a very active social life, and I eventually reconnected to my spiritual life at the Mount Airy Church of God in Christ in Philly with my dear friend, the late Daynese Jimerson

Forsey. During this time, I was still testing my limits in the world. One of the ways I did this was by picking and choosing which biblical principles I wanted to follow and when I would follow them. I had the uneasy feeling that the way I was practicing my spirituality was wrong, but I was able to ignore my feelings and continue on. As my sister often says, "Since the Holy Spirit is a gentleman, he won't interfere when you don't want him to."

I began to pray for God's will to be done in my life, and eventually, my faint feelings of unease grew into a return of my convictions. It was during this time that I began to believe that my spirit had something to share with me, and I listened. I took a year off from dating and partying to focus on my career and my spiritual growth. I stayed as close to the word of God as I could, prayed a lot, sought guidance from my spirit within, and spent more time at home and less "on the scene."

I have had some very significant, very upsetting events in my life. I almost lost my mother in a car accident when I was in 6th grade, I was held up at gunpoint in my apartment when I was in my early 20s, my grandfather died when I was in my mid-20s, and my grandmother died when I was in my mid-30s. I survived all these hard times and came out stronger than I thought possible. Good things were happening to me, and I gave God the glory. I assumed that a continual attitude of gratitude would keep the good times rolling and ensure that I was on the path to easy living.

I was wrong.

Through my mid to late twenties, I worked to develop my spiritual muscles, found love, and got married. But because I didn't have my values in clear view when I got married, I had no clue about how to handle inter-relational value conflicts. I didn't have any examples to follow, and I was living in the LOMB, so I couldn't ask anyone, lest they realize that I was not the "got it all together" woman I tried to show the world. Remember in the LOMB, labels are more important than truth.

I had grown up in a religious environment listening to pastors talk about how God hates divorce and reading this for myself in the Bible, but my marriage wasn't working, and I did not know what to do about it. I was afraid to leave my marriage due to what might happen to my soul, so I stayed even though I was unhappy and my unhappiness was making my family unhappy, too. I began to pray even more often and more earnestly. I needed to hear from God.

I believe spiritual connections begin with your intentions. I know in my heart that God is a loving God, and I believe the words, "'For I know the plans I have for you,' declares the LORD, 'plans to prosper you and not to harm you, plans to give you hope and a future.'"[9] Because of this,

---

9 Jeremiah 29:11

I know that everything will work out for the best. However, that does *not* mean it will be easy.

Knowing this enables me to remain calm in the midst of chaos, to be a light even when darkness is hovering over me, to give emotionally even when I'm spiritually tapped, and to worship even when things are at their worst. On a deep level, I believe him. This journey to truth has caused me to connect with the God I serve in an amazingly authentic way. I represent him, and I pray that I will do so well. The more of him I have in my heart, the less worry I have to take on by myself. This connection has granted for me the sensation of *peace*.

Over the years, I have spent an intense amount of time reflecting, checking in with my soul, praying, and listening; I'm more connected to my spirit and God now than I've ever been. I confess what I believe to be true about me and my journey every day. I expect favor to follow me, and I believe my purpose has been revealed through the process. These beliefs grant me the sensation of *knowing*.

My spirit guides me, and I make every effort to stay present and to listen. I am not a spiritual guru, a religious fanatic, or a believer in condemning others. Being deeply spiritual does not necessarily mean being deeply religious, and it is certainly not limited to Christianity. You can have a strong spiritual life without any belief in a higher power. My belief in God is what works for me. Your job is to find what works for you. I admit that I still work to reconcile my relationship with God with what I was taught to believe. I continue to pray for a deeper relationship and to avoid falling too deep into religious dogma. I'm not here to judge, only to be a light. If others can become connected to their own spirituality in a meaningful way by witnessing my spiritual journey, then my work is done.

* * *

Sprinkling Pepper

"Ask and it will be given to you; seek and you will find; knock and the door will be opened to you."[10] If you're looking, keep searching—not in religion but in the quietness of your soul, in the solemnity of nature, and in the wonder of the world. We are spirits having a human experience. Our souls will know when we have found our way home. Get quiet, and see what you find.

* * *

Chapter 10 Reflections

- Your spiritual walk is personal. Only you can decide which path is right for you.

- Learn to feel comfortable listening to your soul when evaluating your values against the realities of your life.

---

10   Matthew 7:7

- Revisit your spiritual values to ensure your walk and talk are in alignment.

- Your spiritual life should make you feel stronger and happier with your life. If your spirituality is making you miserable, consider re-examining your value alignments.

~ 11 ~

LIVING YOUR EMOTIONAL TRUTH

The Sensation of Feeling

Over the course of a three-year period in the mid-2000s, I experienced a fast and steady stream of emotional truths. During those first three years of this truth journey, I came into the knowledge that I could live an authentic and meaningful life that was true to me. To fully recognize that, however, I had to face the truths I had kept hidden even from myself. What I discovered about myself shocked me to my core. For instance, I had spent my life telling myself and everyone else that certain things simply didn't bother me and that I just had little emotion around them, positive or negative. My actions validated this, as well. I thought that I just lacked a connection and that being emotional didn't register for me. However, what I learned when I started looking inside was that I actually do have emotions!

Until I started really examining my truths, I had always believed my truth was simply that my dad leaving our family when I was five years old had very little effect on me. I was wrong. While I have never been angry with my father for leaving, his absence definitely had an effect. After my father left, my mother never complained, and she held it down like a ninja warrior—what I'm saying is that she didn't fall apart in front of us, *ever*! She never complained about men being "no good." She didn't cry, at least not while we were around. She kept life going, and she didn't ask for help, as far as I knew. I'm not sure if I ever really grieved over my father's leaving us.

So here's the truth that I realized when I began my exploration of my values: Although I never held any ill will for my father, the five-year-old little girl he left never forgot. She was left without warning by someone she knew loved her deeply, and she was given no time to heal.

As I grew, the five-year-old was still in pain, and she made sure I did not allow people to get too close to me. She never forgot that people might leave at any time and for no reason, even if they love you. For most of my life, I was clueless that I felt this way. It wasn't until I began exploring my own truths that I even came close, and a great friend of mine helped me understand more fully by referring me to the book *The Drama of the Gifted Child* by Alice Miller. The book speaks to acknowledging the damage done to us when we're young, even by the most well-intentioned parents. The insights I gained from this book were amazing. I strongly recommend it.

Once I realized I had been unconsciously protecting myself from abandonment, so many aspects of my past relationships began to make sense, including my unsuccessful marriage. While the majority of my relationships ended because of a value misalignment, my lack of attachment played a huge role as well. I looked deeper within myself and examined old friendships, old boyfriends, family members, coworkers, and my feelings about those who had passed on. My goodness, that five-year-old Monica was one strong little girl. She held so much in for so long to protect us both—the younger and older me.

Understanding why I held people at arm's length was a good first step, but the next step was to learn how to let people in and allow myself to attach. It didn't happen all of a sudden. As a matter of fact, I'm still working on it, although I'm so much further. After the value-alignment process of a new relationship, I further judge how things are going by looking at the depth of the feelings I have. I look at each relationship and ask myself, *What would I miss if this person were no longer in my life? Would I miss this person at all?* I take time to process how other hypothetical situations and circumstances regarding this person would make me feel.

Now, as I mentioned in the relationship chapter, not all relationships are created equally. Some have higher balances in your emotional bank account. However, I can usually assess if I'm open to letting someone in by the "miss" factor because this tells me how I value the contribution the person brings to my life, as well as how value aligned we are. This new person should also make that same assessment about me, remembering that function is not enough for sustainability.

I'm not a person who falls apart often. I don't know whether this is because I was born this way or if it was learned along the way; I just don't do it. I believe that the circumstances would have to be pretty extraordinary for me to do so. I attribute some of that to my "anything can happen" philosophy, so maybe my spirit is always at the ready. Despite careful planning, forward thinking, stated commitment, and so forth, life has a way of presenting the most unexpected circumstances. No matter where you are on the emotional spectrum, the way in which you react to a given situation is not necessarily an indicator of how deep your feelings are about the situation. If you're a crier, it is just so. If you are more outwardly less emotional, then you will appear to just soldier on. Some people are somewhere in between.

* * *

Sprinkling Pepper

Sometimes you cry because life dealt you a hard blow; sometimes you cry because you burned your toast. If crying wells up inside you, then you cry. It is what you need to do, and it is a well-known stress reliever. As with everything, though, you have to recognize when it has gone too far. If you can't get out of bed, won't answer phone calls, and start drinking too much too often, then you need to examine your emotional truth, identify where the real problem is, and seek more balance in your life.

* * *

When you are searching for your truth, you want to find out why you behave the way you do in the face of certain situations. Your behavior and your reactions will help you find where the truth lies. Don't worry about which labels society would assign to your various actions or decisions; if the action or decision lines up with your value system, it's your truth. This is not about judgment; it is about identification. Truth is to be acknowledged and examined. Your reaction to your truth can be adjusted when *you* believe it is warranted.

Back in my LOMB days, prior to doing so much truth work, I remember watching shows like *Extreme Makeover: Home Edition*. I would determine how much I believed the people appreciated the makeover based on how emotional and dramatic their reactions were. I'm embarrassed about that now. Not only because it was hypocritical of me—as a not emotionally demonstrative person—to judge others for their lackluster emotional displays, but also because it was judgmental from top to bottom. I can see now that I was judging them based on my own misunderstanding of the way I managed my own emotions. One of the many benefits of learning to recognize my truths is that I can more easily recognize the reasons for my reactions to others' behaviors and adjust accordingly.

To look more closely into your emotional truth, let's explore situational responses that might cause you to have a particular emotion. I'm only touching on a few, so you can use them as examples and think of others that are unique to your life. This should help you to achieve a greater understanding.

Let's say your good friend tells you she will be at your house at 6:00 p.m. She arrives at 7:15 p.m. without any explanation. How does this make you feel? Are you happy to see her? Are you upset because she was late? Maybe it is not a big deal to you because your plans did not require a strict schedule. Maybe it is a big deal, and it doesn't matter what the schedule was. If this would make you feel upset, ask yourself why. If this would not bother you at all, ask yourself why not. Think about the values and sensations that are in the forefront of this situation.

In another example, let's say you tell your manager you're going to complete an assignment and have it to her by 4:00 p.m. At 3:30 p.m., she asks you if the assignment will be done on time. How does this make you feel? Are you happy to have the chance to tell her that everything is on schedule? Are you irritated because she checked up on you? Which of your values triggered these sensations? Are you reacting to the situation in a way that upholds your values?

Lastly, let's imagine that you're in an unfulfilling relationship, and the person breaks up with you. How does this make you feel? Are you relieved or upset? Why do you think you are having that reaction? Think about your values and the sensations that you are having. How are these related to the situation?

Your emotional reactions to various situations have everything to do with your value system and the sensations you're seeking. Remember, some values came about because of our life experiences, some we were born with, and others we accepted from society. For instance, it was important to me to keep people at an emotional distance to minimize being hurt because I'd had the life experience of abandonment. This could also be why I adopted the value of dependability but live by the philosophy that "anything can happen" as a way to keep disappointment in its place. It has served me well under various circumstances in life, particularly in situations that were beyond my control. However, it's not a core value of mine.

If timeliness is one of your top values, then the person who arrives late without calling may cause you to feel angry. The same goes for the other scenarios. If you value dependability, then your manager asking you for something you agreed would be due at a certain time may challenge your value of dependability. Value conflicts are a very common cause of human conflicts.

Understanding your values will assist you greatly in managing your emotions, thoughts, and actions. If we think of the wars, frustrations, and problems of our world, we can probably trace them back to value conflicts and the pursuit of labels.

Having an emotion attached to a value conflict is inevitable, normal, and healthy. How you respond to it will determine your quality of life, particularly when it comes to healthy relationships and your stress level. While mainstream society holds some values in higher regard than others, that doesn't make your values any less valid or true. If you value reliability and lend money to someone who doesn't pay you back, you might feel anger or disappointment. Understanding your values allows you to identify the conflict that has triggered the emotion you're having at any given time; it can also potentially help you to circumvent the relational conflict by communicating with the other person or simply moving forward with understanding.

In addition, the more in tune you are with your values, the better you can manage conflicts and negative emotions before they become a problem. For instance, if you know reliability is a top value for you, then you should communicate that before you loan money to your friend. Remember, people can't live up to your expectations if you never say what they are.

Identifying and understanding your values will not only help you manage emotions but will also assist you in making decisions that benefit your life. If knowledge is something you value greatly, then the goal is to have your choices assist you in realizing that value. On the same note, if you value family, then any decision that diminishes that value will eventually cause you angst and regret.

Values are like a compass. They are great indicators of whether you are living true and heading in the right direction toward your authentic life. The more they show up in the seven areas of your life, the more genuine the journey.

Now that you have more information, be sure to take the time to discover your true values and create your core value list with the "Identifying Your Values Exercise" at the end of the book. Keep narrowing down your core values until you end up with no more than five core values. If you're feeling very ambitious, try to get it down to three. These values will be the ones that evoke the most emotion—the ones you need to be aware of to avoid the pitfalls in how you react. You can manage the emotion by naming it, identifying the value conflict that caused it, and expressing it more appropriately from that point forward.

It will take time to learn to live your emotional truth. It requires deep self-reflection, honesty, and constant monitoring of how you feel about things throughout your life's journey. It also requires that you abandon the pursuit of the "good" labels. While others may try to invalidate your emotions or label your values, you will need to stand firm and remember your reason for taking this journey. Slipping back into the LOMB can happen in the blink of an eye. You have to learn to identify the many indicators of how true you're living emotionally. Let's take a minute to look at a few.

Are you willing to face emotional situations? You must face what you don't want to feel or you cannot grow to understand it.

Are you usually honest with yourself about how you're feeling? When you learn to recognize what you're feeling when you are feeling it, you will be able to move out of the emotional LOMB.

Are you usually honest with others about how you're feeling? While it is not necessary to bare all your feelings to everyone you encounter, your closest friends and family both want and deserve your truth.

Do you believe that emotion is a strength? When you can acknowledge your true sensations to yourself and to your loved ones, you are stronger because you are less likely to be blindsided by your emotions when you have a bad day or experience a vexing situation.

Do you treat yourself kindly? We all make mistakes that cause us to be disappointed with ourselves. By recognizing our own imperfections, we can learn to correct our behavior without anger or resentment.

Without judging yourself, identify how you're feeling along this journey to truth. Have you ever heard people say things like, "I know I shouldn't be upset, but…" or, "I can't believe I'm crying"? Just as in every other area of our lives, we attach labels to emotions. People don't want to let you know they're upset because in our society it can be interpreted as being quick-tempered or too sensitive. People don't want to cry because it has been given the label of weakness in our society. Accepting these limitations on your emotions can create false reactions in situations where holding back is actually communicating something that is not true. Remember that your values are the filter by which you process, and therefore when you have a value confrontation, you will experience an emotion. Don't focus on what the label will be for that truth.

While I believe the world could use a good cry, I'm not advocating that we become a society of tearful interactions. However, I am advocating for the recognition and release of our internal emotions to keep us balanced and authentically moving forward.

* * *

Chapter 11 Reflections

- Give yourself permission to feel and then gain understanding about the root of it.

- Emotions are part of being human.

- Emotional conflict usually comes with value conflict.

- Your emotional truth should be acknowledged and analyzed for understanding.

- No matter what you feel, you're OK, regardless of the labels society may want to assign.

~ 12 ~

LIVING YOUR FINANCIAL TRUTH

The Sensation of Having

Whether you grew up poor, middle class, or wealthy, whether you're a saver or a spender, whether you are now a person with plenty or a person struggling to manage day to day, you have a financial truth. Your internal financial truth may not match your external circumstances, but your financial truth can help you to achieve your financial goals. To learn what your financial truth is, ask yourself why you live the financial life you live. Keep your values on hand to give yourself a point of reference.

There are so many areas to look at when talking about our financial truths. The first place to start is to understand our sensations or feelings about our relationship with money. Many years ago, I read a book by the financial guru Suze Orman in which she asked her readers to reflect on their first memories of money. It was an insightful book. Unfortunately, I didn't get the revelation it offered until later in life; I read it in my twenties when I was completely overspending and felt like the money was endless. My truth then was "I can pay for that." It would be years before I would really understand my financial truth and my values as they related to money. It was a fun, interesting, and stressful journey full of highs and lows.

It was fun because I was often at star-studded events and had so many fun and exciting experiences. I remember dating a young man who would call me at work on a whim and say something like, "Be on the six p.m. train to New York; we're going to the Mary J. Blige concert." After the concert, we would go backstage and hang with all of the people "in the know." I was in my twenties and very excited by that scene then. It was an incredible time, and outside of saving more, I wouldn't have changed a thing. It was interesting because of the people I met. They were from all walks of life with captivating stories. It was stressful because I felt like I had to purchase a new outfit for every event I attended. And it was further stressful because I had to pay for it. Traveling in the entertainment circles and worrying about the labels prompted me to spend way beyond my means.

I am still working on and growing in my own financial truth, even now, so, I cannot point at the "one true way" to your financial life. However, I can share the lessons I've learned from my choices and the unfortunate circumstances in which I've seen others find themselves. You *can* live a life free from worry, one with the freedom to live your truth, even though the pressures of living a certain financial way sometimes cause us to falter in our truth.

I can tell you that if you are in debt, don't make enough to cover your bills and/or have a family and other responsibilities, I understand what you're going through on a very personal level. Some years ago, I was in a similar position. You can come out of your financial struggles; you just have to begin. Begin with an honest assessment of where you are and then write out where you would like to be. Look at your spending every day. Calculate how much it would take to live according to your values. Change what needs to be changed, and keep what needs to be kept without wasting your energy on blaming yourself for your situation. Focus on aligning your financial truth to your values. Seek an advisor or an accountability partner if you need one. It doesn't have to be a professional, especially if money is tight, but it should be someone who will not judge you and can help you explore feasible ways for you to make the most of what you have. If possible, you may have to cut expenses or find a way to generate additional revenue until you can get back on track. Remember, this is your truth and your life. Set yourself up for success.

Regardless of your financial circumstances, whether you are doing well or struggling, living your financial truth as it relates to your values and goals is critical. I can't tell you the list of people I know of who have spent what they made and ended up having to downsize their lifestyles and adjust their truths because the money stopped flowing like it once had. In fact, I'm sure we all know someone who has worked hard to build a comfortable life only to lose it due to health problems, family crisis, divorce, or some other reason.

No matter what you are purchasing, a house, a car, new clothes, or even donations to charity, it's important to understand why you allocate your resources the way you do. You also need to examine if the way you're allocating your money is in line with your values and the life you want. If it is not, what processes or people might help? Living your truth sometimes requires assistance.

Many factors come into play here, such as how to get out of debt, how to use credit cards wisely, how to recover from a financial crisis, what your philanthropic plan should be, and many others that require professional financial advice.

When used in line with your values, money has a way of allowing you to concentrate on the many other facets of your truth. So go live true aesthetically, relationally, spiritually, emotionally, financially, professionally, and parentally.

* * *

Living Your Truth through Special Occasions

Society has a way of interfering with our financial truth by influencing what we do with our money. We also take cues from our upbringing. The level of access to resources while growing up, especially if we had too much or too little, profoundly affects our habits and attitudes toward money.

Our society has built special times into our lives that make living our financial truth more difficult: holidays, birthdays, Valentine's Day, and anniversaries, just to name a few. These are times when many of us spend more than we normally would because we feel pressure to get great presents for our loved ones, and we often put this task off until the last minute. The winter holiday season is the most popular time to slip back into the financial LOMB.

With the endless barrage of ever-multiplying sales catalogs and the social or self-inflicted pressure to give the "best" gifts, the winter holiday season often requires an intense amount of discipline and "value visiting" if we are to stay the course on our financial truth. Set yourself up for a debt-free and stress-free January by creating a budget for your entire holiday spending and stick to it. Be sure to include any food and dessert you need to buy for guests and for making the holiday rounds.

* * *

Sprinkling Pepper
Financial resources and material possessions have a way of making people feel validated. However, it appears that adopting that mindset can lead to constant discontentment and the feeling of never having enough for the next validation. The chase may become pointless. Be careful to align your values with your resources.

* * *

Remember that good gifts don't always have to be expensive.

You're on a journey to living true, and not everyone in your circle will be on this journey with you. Just remember, you don't owe anyone an expensive gift, not even your children and not even if you've given extravagantly in the past. Giving is a choice, not an obligation.

Some of the values that may surface while exploring your financial truth include independence; philanthropy—both to family and to organizations; freedom; and image, just to name a few. When you examine your values, ask yourself why they are important to you. When you can understand the origin of your values, you can make better decisions.

* * *

Chapter 12 Reflections

- No matter what your financial position is, you have a financial truth to live.

- If you are have a secure financially stable life, you still have more freedom to explore how your values can influence the allocation of your money.

- If you want a more secure financial life, you can have it.

- Budget and plan.

- Don't get caught up in winter holiday spending.

~ 13 ~

LIVING YOUR
PROFESSIONAL TRUTH

The Sensation of Purpose

We're going to refer to the terms "job," "profession," and "career" to set up this chapter on living our professional truth. In addition, when I say "professional truth," I'm speaking of the purpose driven occupation you have or want to have. Don't worry if you're not there yet.

When we are children, many adults ask us, "What do you want to be when you grow up?" We're supposed to have an answer. Because of societal clues, we blindly say things like a doctor, or a lawyer, or a teacher, or a firefighter with no regard for what it means to have the job or how we might line it up with our values.

Depending on how we grew up and with whom we were surrounded, we may have chosen a vocation that requires a college degree or one that does not. I went down the path that led to college.

Some of us are clear on the subject we want to major. Others of us are clueless and choose along the way. The majority of us, no matter what we choose or when, have probably been influenced in some way by societal labels about which careers or professions are better than others. Depending on our resolve, we either submit to society's judgments or forge ahead along our own path.

Regardless of our career path, we often start with simple jobs. My first job, for instance, was at a restaurant near my house called Seafood America. I was fifteen years old, and still in high school. I had to get my mother to sign working papers since I wasn't yet sixteen. I worked as a server and sometimes the hostess. It was the most fun job I've ever had. As a server, my primary responsibility was to serve customers. The fun came because I did so alongside some of my best friends and under the management of a twenty-two-year-old young man who was very lenient. I remember laughing a lot, joking around with the cooks, and having little parties on Friday nights.

This is what we do. We start with a simple job. If we are lucky, as I was, we will have a fun job, but it will still be "just a job." It will be a job with responsibilities, perhaps camaraderie, and a paycheck. Our first jobs are rarely the first steps towards our profession or career. For me, at age fifteen, the only reason I had a job was for the money. I wanted to have the power to purchase the things the adults in my life would not.

We start thinking about what we think our future will be from the time we are around seven or eight; that is around the first time we are usually asked, "So, what do you want to be when you grow up?" That question still cracks me up—as if a typical eight-year-old has any real idea. Of course, the point is to encourage children to strive for something, to think about how to be positive, contributing members of society, and it's a great question to jump-start the cogs of the professional mind—as long as the adult realizes that whatever the child picks at age eight may not be the final answer. The growth of one's authentic self takes time and is likely to change several times before the child is an adult.

While I remember being asked the question at an early age, I don't remember the answers I gave until I was in about eighth grade. That was when my math teachers, my mother, my guidance counselor, my friends, my mentors, and I realized that I was good at working through math problems, and I loved it. I liked the decisive nature of math. It has no gray areas; the answer is either x or y, and the reason is clear. Recognizing the decisive person that I am now, I completely understand why I like it. Math doesn't leave you in limbo. It isn't "to be or not to be." "It be," or "it don't." So my answer to the question about my future chosen profession became "to work in finance as a business owner, chief financial officer, or accountant." This answer remained with me all the way through my mid-twenties. I chose accounting because of outside influences, given my love of math. I never even considered how my dislike for routine and my values of variety and creativity might interfere with these goals.

My first job after college was in finance as a health care benefits analyst at a major insurance company. I started in that role and then moved to the auditing department. I managed to do well in the various finance positions I held because I didn't want to fail and because I liked the money—a lot! I was still striving for the sensations of *recognition* and *having*. However, I struggled because I was extremely unfulfilled. This is the result of misaligned values.

The insurance company was a great place to work. It provided great benefits and paid overtime, which I worked plenty of. It invested in employee development and welcomed our input on ways to improve systems and processes. My value of consideration was being met. I "should" have been happy, but I wasn't. I soon realized that I had a misalignment of other critical values. In an earlier chapter, I mentioned that I needed certain things to thrive in my profession: autonomy, problem-solving, variety, creativity, open-mindedness, and consideration. So many of these things were lacking in this otherwise great job, and over time, I became miserable. Staying there was staying in the LOMB.

My boyfriend at the time, who later became my husband, lived in Boston, so after a year of managing a long-distance relationship, I moved there and began working at an off-price retail conglomerate. It was a nice introduction to Boston, and I was able to grow professionally. I met three of my mentors, Amy Fardella, Virginia Nelson, and Jerome Smalls, at this company while I continued in my finance career. I began working in the auditing department, and then transitioned to financial planning and analysis. I also worked a short time in human resources before ending in accounting management. I was fortunate to work for a company that invested in its employees, allowed me the freedom to explore other professions within the company, and wanted to help me be successful. However, I eventually became bored with the routine of my positions in finance and the lack of creativity allowed in those roles, as well as the absence of other values.

I moved on. This time I landed at a fitness shoe and apparel company, in another finance position. I eventually transitioned from this company to an operations position at one of the top commercial real estate firms in Massachusetts. You may remember the discussion from Chapter 4 about my dissatisfaction in the finance profession. Suffice it to say, I had to bump up against my value system quite a few times in my professional life before I realized that the problem was not with the individual jobs but with the profession itself. It just did not suit me.

I did not take a hard look at my values until I was considering a transition from my role as head of operations to commercial real estate broker. Brokerage held an opportunity for me to explore some of my values of autonomy, problem-solving, variety, consideration, creativity, and open-mindedness, and I could make a significant contribution to the bottom line. I thought I had found the right position for me; unfortunately, the sensations and presence of a few of my values blinded me to one extremely important point: I had very little interest in office space. In time, I realized I wasn't interested in a long-term career discussing and negotiating office space. My core values ultimately won the battle.

I left commercial real estate to run my current company, Monica Cost Enterprises, a firm that facilitates the creation of values-based pathways by utilizing our groundbreaking Value Identification Process™ (V.I.P.) to increase organizational effectiveness, individual fulfillment, and entrepreneurial success through workshop facilitation, keynotes, consulting, and brand strategy. I'm the boss—*autonomy.* I work when I choose at all times of the day and night and no two days are the same—*variety.* I always have a new question to answer—*problem solving.* I meet new people all year long— *variety.* I am challenged to think outside of the box—*creativity and open-mindedness.* I am invited to speak at various events—*consideration.* Finally, and most importantly, I get to do it all while helping my clients to be authentic— *problem-solving again.*

In addition to belonging, I believe that self-preservation—with purpose and passion—may just be one of the most common human pursuits around profession. My cousins, friends, and I were taught from a very young age to make our own path in the world so that we would be self-sufficient. Although we were asked what we'd like to be when we grew up, we were simultaneously encouraged to choose professions that were considered the "good" ones, the ones that were more in line with what society valued as respected professions. We were encouraged to be doctors, lawyers, athletes, Wall Street brokers, or business owners; we were expected to want to be "superstars" in the positions that our society considers "great." Those careers are noble and worth pursuing, but only when they line up with your values, your concept of who you are, and your vision for your life.

Adults, no matter how well intentioned, often don't pay attention to children's values or the things that really matter to them. They usually encourage them to choose the "hot jobs." Even if you have skills that line up with one of the chosen professions, that doesn't automatically mean it will be a fulfilling career. It is still necessary to understand the environment, the aspects, and the elements of the career you are choosing to ensure value alignment.

Research has shown for some time now that the United States may be in trouble due to a talent shortage. We're not graduating enough students in the science, technology, engineering, and math fields. We need to start paying attention to students' interests during their formative years instead of forcing them to learn how to pass one-size-fits-all standardized tests. I believe that if each child were encouraged to examine his or her own core—without the biased influence from educators, parents, and others based on age, race, gender, and so forth—we would have a surplus of bright, imaginative, and excited young adults ready to fill that talent shortage.

* * *

Sprinkling Pepper
Your career path choice should be hinged on the things you care about, not what's expected of you. I know

doctors who are now teachers, Wall Street brokers who are now in the Peace Corps, and lawyers who are now singers—not because they had a change in their value systems but because they had never acknowledged their values in the first place.

* * *

My company began as a personal brand company. I took notice and was interested in very knowledgeable professionals who were, for some reason, not advancing in their careers. After looking deeper into the situation, I realized this problem was usually related to how they thought of themselves in context to their professional environment, how they presented themselves professionally, and the lack of understanding about how they were being experienced. Today we call this "personal brand." It is comprised of our appearance, communication style and content, character, and reputation.

My original work primarily examined these elements and formalized ways to improve on them in every area for career advancement. However, I soon realized that addressing these areas without an understanding of the individual's personal values was a setup for a future that would be unfulfilling. It would actually assist people in remaining in the LOMB by helping them create a market-led brand that would fit the role, versus a value-led brand that would ensure their place in the LOAT. That's a key point.

It is difficult, though, to resist striving for the sought-after position, the one that delivers the most sensations of *acceptance*, *superiority*, *recognition*, and more. However, if you can keep revisiting your values and seeking understanding about your desired sensations, you can position yourself into a career that is both fulfilling and based on your value system.

I know of many people who took a position primarily for the money. There was no analysis or aligning of values. As I mentioned earlier, we are not taught to analyze our values in our society. Eventually the misaligned values were evident and the unfulfillment of the position became clear, causing a need for change.

In the midst of identifying your professional values, do not ignore the power of passion. Passion comes from the subjects and interests you could talk about and engage in all day. They bring you joy and give you the opportunity to flex your mental muscles. When your values are at play and your interests are piqued, you can slip very easily into finding your purpose.

I believe our purpose transcends our professional lives. It's who we are at the core all the time. For instance, if an aspect of your purpose is to troubleshoot, you do it in every area of your life. People may call you a complainer, but you know that you're really good at identifying things that don't fit and figuring out how to fix them. If you are a creator, then you fill this role not just at work but also at home and in your social activities as well. When a problem arises, you automatically begin creating solutions that are outside of the box. Your purpose finds a way to show up.

* * *

Changing Your Professional Truth

I know from personal experience how exciting and even scary changing careers can be. I went from finance to real estate to running my own consulting firm. Since many of us are brought up under the current system of valuing certain professions and chasing the labels, it is completely normal to find ourselves in a profession that we simply do not like.

No matter how old you are, you can always change your circumstances. What you may want to consider is this: How much is it worth to you to get out? And what's your real reason for wanting out? Ask yourself if you want out because of value-alignment issues, work environment, job opportunities, growth opportunities, paycheck restrictions, or just a lack of interest. Maybe it is something else entirely. If you've discovered you're truly not cut out for your current profession because of a value misalignment and you're willing to make sacrifices for the sake of having a value-aligned career, then it's time to get moving.

Here are some steps to take to make the change so you can begin living your professional truth:

1. Don't jump too quickly.

2. Be kind to yourself. Do not beat yourself up for not having pursued a certain career, started a business, gone back to school when you had the chance, or so forth. Start now!

3. Gain a complete understanding of your values and identify your desired sensations. This will help you to avoid jumping into a similar situation where you will be unsatisfied again.

4. Reflect on your current position to determine if there is a way to introduce your values and sensations into this role. What's missing? What would it take to find it in your current profession?

5. Take time to assess your current personal brand in the marketplace by getting feedback from others about your brand. Ask five to seven people to describe your appearance, communication style, character, and reputation. Give them permission to be tactfully honest.

6. Don't judge the feedback you receive or the labels it may seem to convey about you. Own your strengths, and look closely at any areas

where you need polishing. Use what you learn to make authentic adjustments in any other areas.

7. Get a mentor—actually get a few. Mentors of varying backgrounds add amazing color to your life by helping you see the world from a multitude of angles. They are not there to tell you what to do but rather to give you guidance and share their journeys for your edification and growth.

8. Think about a few subject matters that pique your interest—things that you could talk or learn about all day. This evaluation will assist you in landing in a place where you can hone your purpose and passion because your connection is from the heart, not from external sources.

9. Do your due diligence in researching the profession(s) you believe you want to go into. Find people who do and love what you want to do. Ask a lot of questions. Shadow someone in the profession, if possible. Determine if your values will be met in the profession.

10. Tune out the external voices and societal pressures around what's a good, noble, and worthy career. While you're living up to their expectations, your truth is being further buried in the LOMB, and you're delaying your own ultimate personal fulfillment.

11. Once you decide on a new profession, research various companies and/or opportunities where you can work in your new profession.

12. Do a quick search on how your new profession is doing in the marketplace. See what new developments have come about. This will have an impact on how you proceed in your chosen area. If your chosen career is on the decline, find out how what you want to do is currently being done so you can adjust.

13. If you're transitioning to an organization, be sure to check in with the environment to ensure that they live your values and that it is right for you.

14. As a new or recommitted LYTES, be sure you don't fall into the LOMB by judging other people's truths. Let's support one another in this journey as we travel along.

* * *

Because we spend so much of our lives pursuing our professions and careers, having purpose and passion around them could shift us into a wonderful LOAT.

* * *

Chapter 13 Reflections

• Self-preservation, with purpose and passion are critical.

- Values have as much to do with your profession as they do with every other area of your life.

- If you learn your values aren't being met in your current profession, look into finding ways to change that.

- Don't be afraid to admit you don't like your profession, no matter how much other people say you should.

- Look for purpose and passion in your profession.

- If you're making a career change, don't omit revisiting your values.

~ 14 ~

LIVING YOUR PARENTAL TRUTH

The Sensation of Imparting

Guiding people through the process of raising their children is taboo in our society. In addition, there is no one "right" way to parent. Although we know that babies come with a pretty large list of responsibilities, we tend to bristle when someone offers unsolicited advice. Because of this, we also avoid giving advice to others if we see them making what we believe is a bad call in parenting. In our society, we are obligated to feed, change, and love our babies, but we are also charged with ensuring that these little humans grow up to be well-adjusted, caring, self-initiating, civic-minded, and healthy individuals who will contribute positively to society. And we do not even have a certified manual on the subject! We can only reference our own upbringing, look at examples of others' experiences, and study expert research.

Just to be clear, I am neither a child psychologist nor an expert on the subject. My credentials for parenting advice are no better than anyone else's: I am a mom, a friend, an aunt, and a cousin. I have observed my own children, other people's children, and I have lived long enough to know adults that I once knew as children. I pay close attention to the results.

If you want to live authentically, then it is likely that you want an authentic life for your children as well. You want to set up a life of truth and honesty for them to see demonstrated and hear communicated on a daily basis. This will help them to live more authentically when they are young and will prevent them from having to be reeducated about their truths when they are older. I believe this will set them up to have higher levels of confidence and self-esteem. It will impart the sensation of assuredness.

Most children have the ability to develop in all academic areas to varying levels of proficiency. Striving for perfection isn't the goal and actually does not provide any indication of success. But if better is possible, then good isn't enough. Confidence in any area of our life comes from trying something and being successful, or at least coming out knowing more than we did before. It doesn't mean we didn't fail along the way; it just means we ultimately implemented a strategy that worked. One of my favorite quotes on this subject comes from Dr. Jeff Howard of the Efficacy Institute, who says, "Failure is not an indication of your ability, just a need to adjust your strategy." That's powerful learning. When I first heard it, I had to take a moment to digest it. It applies not only to raising children but also to every other area of life where we have an opportunity for growth in some desired result.

Your kids should be able to try and fail; it will help them to gain more confidence. If your three-year-old daughter tries to pour her own juice and spills it, you have an instant to decide whether to praise the effort or to scold the result. Your decision will have an impact on whether she tries to expand her skills or sits back in fear of making a mistake going forward. If you recognize the child's effort and not the outcome, you might say something about the things your daughter did correctly and add an idea that might make it easier the next time. This response gives your child the assurance that you believe in her ability to do it and encourages her to develop another strategy. This can apply to so many areas of your child's life. Some of the most amazing work around this confidence-building subject comes from the Efficacy Institute. Check it out at Efficacy.org. The information presented there is changing lives, including mine.

As I have mentioned before, I was raised in a single-parent household with my mother and younger sister. My mother was a phenomenal parent by my account. She poured affection, confidence, curiosity, self-awareness, strength, high self-regard, a get-it-done attitude, and more into us. We had many ups and downs, emotionally and financially, but my mother always seemed to know how to help us process and move forward.

Out of love and consideration, my mother didn't always make us finish everything we started, especially if we didn't really want to. I often wonder if I would have become a great gymnast if I'd stuck with it after I fell off the balance beam at a gymnastics meet or if I would have been a great track star if I hadn't quit once I learned that track meets were at 6:00 a.m. I know my mother meant well by letting me quit these activities, but later in life, I had to learn to overcome the hurdle of wanting to quit before finishing a task.

In college, I turned around this behavior of quitting something interesting once it becomes hard. I learned to drop some classes and push through others. Eventually, I completed my college education and my pledge process.

I'm not perfect, and I'm actually not even striving for perfection. I'm a well-adjusted work in progress. One of the most important things my mother instilled in me is confidence. I truly believe that ultimately everything will work out. What I don't know, I can learn; the rest goes into my prayers.

I am raising two amazing boys, who will one day be adult men. They are learning what it means to be, good friends to others, considerate teammates, and positive contributors to the world, but they are in no way perfect. Their father—my former husband—and I are supporting them in establishing their spiritual connection, understanding their emotional sensations, and identifying their values. When they are having feelings or emotions, they are free to express them respectfully. No matter how they are feeling, I don't try to convince them it's not a big deal. We all know how it feels when we tell our significant other or someone else how we feel about something, only to be told something like, "Oh, give me a break—you let that bother you?" or "Don't be sad over that little thing." We don't like it because we realize that our feelings have just been dismissed as not valuable. Children are little people, and they have their own values. They do not like it any more than we do when their feelings are devalued.

My former husband and I are executing our mission to give our boys the tools they will need to have the best human experience possible. It will not be exempt from pain, process, or hard learning, but it will be filled with love, acceptance, and affirmation.

Although I'm not a child psychologist, I do have some suggestions that have helped me while raising my children:

1. Be honest with yourself about your children. If they exhibit behaviors that are destructive, physically or verbally, getting a handle on those behaviors now rather than spend time explaining them away will serve your children well. While you may be afraid that confronting their faults may damage your parent-child relationship, changing these behaviors early will set your children up for greater levels of success later.

2. Children actually desire and prefer boundaries. Letting your children run wild, break their toys, eat as much sugar as they want, and swear at you isn't the way to let them establish independence. Those actions are a cry for help, a chance given to the parents to show they actually care. Show your children that you love them by helping them to

understand the reasons for the boundaries. This will allow them to know the difference between those boundaries that can be pushed and challenged and those that are established for their well-being. It is appropriate for your child to say "No" to you in a reasonable tone and for a good reason, but it is not appropriate for your child to scream "NO" at you when you are making a reasonable demand.

3. Remember that you are raising someone's friend, husband, wife, coworker, neighbor, community leader, manager, CEO, or president. Be mindful what you're showing and teaching them. The way in which we treat, respond to, and guide our children assists in creating the adults they turn out to be.

4. Don't transfer your problems onto your children. It's impossible to go through life without any emotional wounds. Without being intentional about our healing, we can keep these wounds forever. When we experience our children going through something that takes the scab off or irritates our wounds, we may react to it from our own perspective and not the truth of our children. We must remember that they have their own path. The first step is to understand how they are experiencing the situation and not to project our own feelings on to them.

5. If you're divorced, separated, or otherwise not with your children's other parent, please make every effort to cooperate and get along for your

children's sake. Take the high road even when your co-parent does not. Your children are learning how to become themselves by watching and listening to you. In addition, they will need tools to navigate this world for themselves. Set them up for success by showing them that you can parent together—while apart.

6. Teach your children that quicker doesn't mean smarter and that smart is something you get, not something you are. Once you have knowledge, it doesn't matter how long it took you to obtain it. If you only praise them and tell them how smart they are when they are quick or correct, then they may think of themselves as failures when it takes them more time or they get it wrong. Praise the effort, not the results.

7. Assist your children in living their truth. Remember that your children's truths may differ from yours; help them to understand that this is okay. You can mold them, shape them, and feed your truth to them all you like, but ultimately, their truth will prevail. This could also save you money on therapy later on.

8. Encourage them to communicate respectfully with you no matter how they are feeling. When they do, don't try to invalidate or explain away their feelings. Some of the topics may be tough for you to discuss, but be strong and let them talk to you. If you have to, ask questions to be sure you understand. Your

children want to be able to trust you. You will be amazed at the new depths of your relationship with your children once they learn that they can.

* * *

Chapter 14 Reflections

- Children have their own values.

- Don't expect your children to have the exact same values that you have.

- When it come to your children, make every effort to stick with the facts and refuse to label them.

- Build confidence in your children.

- Pay attention to the effort.

~ 15 ~

SENSATION CONTINUATION

Go Forward in Truth

We have now covered the basics and more to help you move out of the LOMB and into the LOAT. I hope that you are more aware of your desired sensations, have gained a clear understanding of the importance of identifying your values, achieved a pinpointed location of yourself in relation to those values, and feel enthusiastic to move forward in truth.

Each area we discussed requires a core value identification and a sensation alignment. Finding your truth in the various areas of your life will take some time. You can start by utilizing the Truth Positioning System (TPS) at the end of this book. You may find that you are living true in some areas but not so in others. This is where your values will be your guide. Once you've identified your values, then you can use them as a road map to your destination—aesthetically, relationally, spiritually, emotionally, financially, professionally, and parentally.

We're at the beginning of a journey that will lead us to authenticity. As people see us living our truths and moving out of the LOMB, they will see us building a place where everyone's gifts, talents, and positions in this world are celebrated, where children are not mocked for marching to the beat of their own drummer, and adults don't feel compelled to keep real estate in the LOMB. While it is not necessary to convert everyone in your path to your value system, it is also not necessary for you to feel like an outcast for living your truth.

It will often be tempting to slip back into inauthentic living in the LOMB. Someone may make a comment, suggest a label for your behavior, or otherwise encourage you to make adjustments against your value system to conform. You may comply with those suggestions because something about the situation may make you feel that your value isn't held in high regard. You may see an advertisement on television encouraging you to shop when your financial truth dictates that you don't. You might stumble across a great person who really excites you in some way and be tempted to dive in headfirst instead of checking first for the value alignment. I couldn't begin to name all the temptations that will sneak up on you or those that will throw themselves at your feet. The best way to deal with these temptations is to make sure that you are careful and that you have the support of other LYTES (Live-Your-Truth Experience Soldiers). Keep your values close to your heart to avoid being sucked back into the LOMB.

Even now, after all this time working on living my truth, I have had to resist the temptation of slipping back into the LOMB. It is not easy, and we all have triggers that threaten to undo all our hard work, but with determination and the support of our friends, we can live in the LOAT.

Here are a few steps so you can begin living your truth today:

1. Complete the "Identifying Your Values Exercise" at the end of this book. You can begin to understand your values by looking at what things upset you, what subjects you feel strongly about, what you need in your life for fulfillment, and so forth.

2. Find an accountability partner. Have your partner read this book as well so that you are both using the same language and points of reference.

3. Learn to refrain from labeling others. We don't want to label others, and we don't want others to label us.

4. Look at each of the seven areas and identify your values in each. They may be the same as your overall values, or they may vary.

5. Refuse to give in to the pressure to be what you are not.

Congratulations on beginning your journey to truth! I appreciate the opportunity to support you and pray you will continue the good work you've started.

Live your truth!

**THE JOURNEY OF A THOUSAND MILES
BEGINS WITH ONE STEP.
~ LAO TZU**

Congratulations on Beginning Your Journey!

THE LYTE PLEDGE
(although not to be taken lightly)

I realize that it takes the complete functioning of all authentic value systems to ensure that our world is at its best. I understand that we are one people with common goals and a desire to live our most fulfilling and authentic lives. In this place, we can be the best and therefore give our best. I understand that living my truth is the path to a fulfilling life.

If you agree, please take the Live Your Truth Experience Pledge.

THE THINGS I USED TO DO TO SNEEZE

I,   , pledge

- To live my life in the LOAT from this point forward, earnestly seeking out and living by my most authentic values

- To replace society's values with my own

- To leave labeling to those who live in the LOMB

- To make decisions based upon truth and not perception

- To accept my values and respect the values of others

- To understand that a misalignment of values only gives me information to make decisions, not the right to judge others or to label them

——   ——

Signature   Date

VALUE IDENTIFICATION EXERCISE

1. Get a pen, pencil, crayon, or marker, and a piece of paper, cardboard, smart board, or something else to record on.

2. Think about situations or circumstances that upset you, embarrass you, scare you, make you feel bad, or otherwise put you in a really bad emotional space. In essence, I'm asking you to identify your major pet peeves. These could range from someone cutting you off in traffic to someone telling lies, from gossipers to self-absorbed people. I mean anything that triggers a major negative response in you. Write these situations down in simple sentences. Don't label the situations or yourself for being negatively impacted by them! Narrow your list down to the top five upsetting circumstances. Leave room on your paper for the next step.

   Example: when someone passes judgment on me or someone else, when people are loud in public, being given only one option on how to do something, when someone draws conclusions without enough information, inappropriate behavior exhibited by others or myself, when I make a poor presentation of myself.

3. Read through the list of values at the end of this section and make a note of any that resonate

with you. While reading through them, keep the pet peeves you list above in mind. Remember, don't worry about any label associated with the value!

Example: Consideration, options, flexibility, problem-solving, creativity, etc.

4. You probably have many values noted. Go through the ones you noted and pare them down again. The goal is to get to your top five.

5. Look over the seven areas of life that I talked about in the book. Do your top five values hold true for each area of your life, or do you have different values depending on which aspect of your life you are dealing with? The goal is to have your true top five values hold true in every area of your life.

Values List

Below is a list of a great many values that you may relate to. Go through this list and copy down the values that you best relate to. You could make a copy of this list, then cut it into squares to make piles of values that you can further sort to help you narrow down your core values.

Abundance	Acceptance	Accessibility	Accomplishment
Accuracy	Achievement	Acknowledgment	Activeness
Adaptability	Adoration	Adventure	Affection
Aggressiveness	Agility	Alertness	Altruism
Ambition	Amusement	Anticipation	Appreciation
Approachability	Assertiveness	Assurance	Attentiveness
Attractiveness	Audacity	Availability	Awareness
Awe	Balance	Beauty	Being the Best
Belonging	Bliss	Boldness	Bravery
Brilliance	Calmness	Camaraderie	Candor
Capability	Care	Carefulness	Celebrity
Certainty	Challenge	Charity	Charm
Chastity	Cheerfulness	Clarity	Cleanliness
Clear Mindedness	Cleverness	Closeness	Comfort
Commitment	Compassion	Completion	Composure
Concentration	Conformity	Congruency	Connection
Consciousness	Consideration	Consistency	Contentment
Continuity	Contribution	Control	Conviction
Coolness	Cooperation	Cordiality	Correctness
Courage	Courtesy	Craftiness	Creativity
Credibility	Cunning	Curiosity	Daring
Decisiveness	Decorum	Deference	Delight

Dependability	Depth	Desire	Determination
Devotion	Devoutness	Dignity	Diligence
Direction	Directness	Discipline	Discovery
Discretion	Diversity	Dominance	Dreaming
Drive	Duty	Eagerness	Education
Effectiveness	Elation	Elegance	Empathy
Encouragement	Endurance	Energy	Enjoyment
Entertainment	Enthusiasm	Excellence	Excitement
Exhilaration	Expectancy	Expediency	Experience
Expertise	Exploration	Expressiveness	Extravagance
Extroversion	Exuberance	Fairness	Faith
Fame	Family	Fascination	Fashion
Fearlessness	Ferocity	Fidelity	Fierceness
Financial Independence	Firmness	Fitness	Flexibility
Focus	Fortitude	Frankness	Freedom
Friendliness	Frugality	Fun	Generosity
Giving	Grace	Gratitude	Gregariousness
Growth	Guidance	Happiness	Harmony
Health	Heart	Helpfulness	Heroism
Holiness	Honesty	Honor	Hopefulness
Hospitality	Humility	Humor	Hygiene
Imagination	Impact	Impartiality	Independence
Industry	Ingenuity	Inquisitiveness	Insightfulness
Inspiration	Integrity	Intelligence	Intensity
Introversion	Intuition	Intuitiveness	Inventiveness
Investing	Joy	Judiciousness	Justice
Keenness	Kindness	Knowledge	Leadership
Learning	Liberation	Liberty	Liveliness
Logic	Longevity	Looking Good	Love

Loyalty	Making a Difference	Mastery	Maturity
Meekness	Mellowness	Meticulousness	Mindfulness
Modesty	Motivation	Mysteriousness	Nature
Neatness	Nerve	Obedience	Open-mindedness
Openness	Optimism	Order	Organization
Originality	Passion	Peace	Perceptiveness
Perfection	Perkiness	Perseverance	Persistence
Persuasiveness	Philanthropy	Playfulness	Pleasantness
Pleasure	Poise	Polish	Popularity
Potency	Power	Practicality	Pragmatism
Precision	Preparedness	Presence	Privacy
Proactivity	Professionalism	Prosperity	Prudence
Punctuality	Purity	Realism	Reason
Reasonableness	Recognition	Recreation	Relaxation
Reliability	Religiousness	Resilience	Resolve
Resourcefulness	Respect	Rest	Restraint
Reverence	Richness	Rigor	Ritual
Sacredness	Satisfaction	Security	Self-control
Self-reliance	Sensitivity	Sensuality	Serenity
Service	Sexuality	Sharing	Shrewdness
Silence	Silliness	Simplicity	Sincerity
Skillfulness	Solidarity	Solitude	Soundness
Speed	Spirit	Spirituality	Spontaneity
Spunk	Stability	Stealth	Stillness
Strength	Structure	Success	Support
Supremacy	Surprise	Sympathy	Synergy
Teamwork	Thankfulness	Thoroughness	Thoughtfulness
Thrift	Tidiness	Timeliness	Traditionalism
Tranquility	Transcendence	Trust	Trustworthiness

Truth	Understanding	Uniqueness	Unity
Usefulness	Utility	Valor	Variety
Victory	Vigor	Virtue	Vision
Vitality	Warmth	Watchfulness	Wealth
Willfulness	Willingness	Winning	Wisdom
Wittiness	Wonder	Youthfulness	Zeal

TRUTH-POSITIONING SYSTEM
(TPS)

Pet Peeves	Values

TRUTH-POSITIONING SYSTEM
(TPS)

Make copies of this card and put it where you can see it often. You will be amazed by how much a little understanding about who you are can help to clarify your decision-making process throughout each day. This card is intended to inspire healthy conversations with yourself and to help map your continued journey in the Land of Authenticity and Truth.

NOTES

NOTES

NOTES

NOTES

ABOUT THE AUTHOR

Monica Cost, a Philadelphia native, is a brand strategist, author, inspirational speaker, advocate for authentic living, and co-parent of two young men with her former husband. She runs The Core Value Company, a firm dedicated to providing value aligned solutions for organizations around human development and authentic brand solutions, as well as for individuals around life and professional strategy. She has over seventeen years of experience in brand development, public speaking, and communications. She has worked with many notable celebrities, Fortune 500 corporations, and non-profit organizations. Ms. Cost was awarded the prestigious 40 Under 40 Award by the *Boston Business Journal* and the Girl Scouts Leading Woman Award. Cost has also been recognized in the *Boston Herald* as one of "the Hub's (Boston's) Future Leaders," in the *Boston Globe* for becoming the first black female commercial real estate broker in Massachusetts, and in *Women's Business Boston* for being an emerging leader. In addition, she was interviewed and featured in The History Makers project (Thehistorymakers. com). She is a columnist for the celebrity news site, EUR

Web and is frequently quoted on various celebrity news sites. In her leisure time, she enjoys self-reflecting, reading, watching movies, traveling, shopping, meeting new people, gathering with friends, and mentoring. One of her favorite quotes is "For as he thinketh in his heart, so is he."[11]

---

11 Proverbs 23:7

APPENDIX

- Monica Cost, pathfinding and strategy firm creating brand congruency through authentic brand solutions: www.monicacost.com

- CJ Miller, author and TV personality. *Grind: How to Turn Your Coffee Break into Your Big Break*

- Kevon Edmonds, vocalist

Special Thanks to:
- To my editor, **Veronica Tuggle**, who took such amazing care and had so much patience with me and with this project. You came at just the right time. Your connection to this work, attention to detail, calm spirit, and encouraging communications made this possible. I have never gone through this process before, but I cannot think of a more qualified person to have walked with me through this part of the journey.

- All the people who wrote and called to express the impact this offering has had on their lives. You are too many to name, but my heart is encouraged.

217

Contact Information
Web: www.monicacost.com
Email: liveyourtruth@monicacost.com
Facebook: Monica Hairston Cost
Twitter: @monicacost
Bookings & Media: liveyourtruth@monicacost.com